WHY READ WOLLSTONECRAFT TODAY?

What relevance does Mary Wollstonecraft's thought have today? In this insightful book, Sandrine Bergès engages Wollstonecraft with contemporary social and political issues, demonstrating how this pioneering eighteenth-century feminist philosopher addressed concerns that resonate strongly with those faced by twenty-first-century feminists. Wollstonecraft's views on oppression, domination, gender, slavery, social equality, political economics, health, and education underscore her commitment to defending the rights of all who are oppressed. Her ideas shed light on challenges we face in social and political philosophy, including intersectionality, health inequalities, universal basic income, and masculinity. Clear and accessible, this book is an invaluable resource for students and anyone interested in discovering who Mary Wollstonecraft was and how her ideas can help us navigate the struggles of today's feminist movement.

SANDRINE BERGÈS is British Academy Global Professor in the Department of Philosophy, University of York and Professor Department of Philosophy, Bilkent University. She has written books and articles on women in the history of philosophy, including Mary Wollstonecraft, Sophie de Grouchy, and Olympe de Gouges.

WHY READ THEM TODAY?

The books in this series offer new interpretations of thinkers who in different ways reward contemporary re-examination, showing how their thought is particularly relevant to us today.

Books in This Series

STEVEN NADLER, *Why Read Maimonides Today?*

SANDRINE BERGÈS, *Why Read Wollstonecraft Today?*

YUVAL AVNUR, *Why Read Pascal Today?*

WHY READ WOLLSTONECRAFT TODAY?

SANDRINE BERGÈS

Bilkent University and University of York

CAMBRIDGE
UNIVERSITY PRESS

Shaftesbury Road, Cambridge CB2 8EA, United Kingdom

One Liberty Plaza, 20th Floor, New York, NY 10006, USA

477 Williamstown Road, Port Melbourne, VIC 3207, Australia

314–321, 3rd Floor, Plot 3, Splendor Forum, Jasola District Centre,
New Delhi – 110025, India

103 Penang Road, #05–06/07, Visioncrest Commercial, Singapore 238467

Cambridge University Press is part of Cambridge University Press & Assessment,
a department of the University of Cambridge.

We share the University's mission to contribute to society through the pursuit of
education, learning and research at the highest international levels of excellence.

www.cambridge.org
Information on this title: www.cambridge.org/9781009360036
DOI: 10.1017/9781009360067

© Sandrine Bergès 2026

This publication is in copyright. Subject to statutory exception and to the provisions
of relevant collective licensing agreements, no reproduction of any part may take
place without the written permission of Cambridge University Press & Assessment.

When citing this work, please include a reference to the DOI 10.1017/9781009360067

First published 2026

A catalogue record for this publication is available from the British Library

A Cataloging-in-Publication data record for this book is available from the Library of Congress

ISBN 978-1-009-36003-6 Hardback
ISBN 978-1-009-36004-3 Paperback

Cambridge University Press & Assessment has no responsibility for the persistence
or accuracy of URLs for external or third-party internet websites referred to in this
publication and does not guarantee that any content on such websites is, or will remain,
accurate or appropriate.

For EU product safety concerns, contact us at Calle de José Abascal, 56, 1°, 28003 Madrid,
Spain, or email eugpsr@cambridge.org

Contents

Acknowledgements		*page* vi
1	Defender of Rights	1
2	Standing Up for All the Oppressed	19
3	The Caged Life	39
4	The Body	61
5	Happy Families	80
6	Working for a Living	97
7	Philosophy, Progress, and Real Politics	114
8	Where Will the Men Go?	134
References		142
Index		150

Acknowledgements

This book could not have come into existence without the large group of Wollstonecraft scholars I have been working with over the past five years. We first met in San Francisco in 2019, then in Boston in 2021, and then online in 2022, at a series of workshops we called 'Wollapalooza', organized by Alan Coffee, Eileen Hunt, and myself. They were Lena Halldenius, Martina Reuter, Karen Green, Laura Brace, Helen McCabe, Nancy Kendrick, Penny Weiss, Ruth Abbey, Wendy Gunther-Canada, Natalie Taylor, Daniel I. O'Neill, Elizabeth Frazer, Sylvana Tomaselli and Virginia Sapiro, Megan Gallagher, Wayne Bodle, Carol Bensick, Manjeet Ramgotra, Karie Cross Riddle, Stefan Wheelock, Gozde Yildirim, Sarah Bonfim, Serena Vantin, Adam Lebovitz, Allauren Forbes, Serena Mocci, Federica Falchi, Lorna Bracewell, Madeline Cronin, Emily Dumler-Winckler, Spyridon Tegos, Alea Henle, Wendy Gunther-Canada, Lisa Pace Vetter, Alvin B. Tillery, Jack Turner, and Garrett FitzGerald. Together, we became the Mary Wollstonecraft Philosophical Society, and we worked on publications, including the *Wollstonecraftian Mind*. It is a joy to list the names of so many people who have been dedicated to working on Wollstonecraft over the past years, and knowing that I am still forgetting some.

There is also an older group, subsumed under the larger one, but which deserves special mention. We first met ten years ago in Lund, where Lena Halldenius invited Martina Reuter, Alan Coffee, and myself for a small workshop. We have been meeting and collaborating ever since, and their support over the years has meant everything to my understanding of Wollstonecraft's work. I hope that they don't regret my saying that after they read this book!

Two people read most of the chapters in draft: Alan Coffee and Bill Wringe. I hope they think I did their comments justice. I would also like to thank my graduate students, who discussed Wollstonecraft's works with me in our reading group while I was writing this: Bengü Demirtaş, Eylül Yücel, and Sena Çiftci. Their insights really helped me rethink what it means to read Wollstonecraft today.

CHAPTER I

Defender of Rights

In the Unitarian chapel of Newington Green, where dissenting minister Richard Price once gave his sermons, hangs a plaque to one of Price's friends and followers: Mary Wollstonecraft. The plaque reads 'philosopher, human rights pioneer, travel writer, educationalist'. Mary Wollstonecraft was all that. She was a philosopher who wrote treatises and interacted with the best thinkers of her time in England and France: Richard Price himself, Thomas Paine, Catherine Macaulay and William Godwin, Condorcet, Brissot, and Madame Roland. She wrote about the human rights of the poor in France, of the enslaved Africans in the colonies, of women, and of children. She produced philosophical, literary, and journalistic writings about her travels to Ireland, Portugal, France, and Scandinavia. And she wrote several books on education, in particular on the education of women: a short treatise, a book of educational stories, a reader for young women, and an unfinished book of lessons for her daughters, and of course, a large part of the *Vindication of the Rights of Woman* is about education.

Mary Wollstonecraft was all that the plaque says, but she was more: she was a novelist who published two novels (one unfinished), she was a political journalist and historian who produced texts on the development and on the early history of the French Revolution. And, as I will argue (and clarify) throughout this volume, she was a feminist.

Wollstonecraft was a fascinating writer whose life and works make for great biographies. But should we read her now as a philosopher? After all, her husband, William Godwin, was better known as a philosopher during his lifetime, and not many read him now. Her mentors Richard Price and Catherine Macaulay are mostly forgotten; their philosophical works are difficult to find. So why should Wollstonecraft be any different, and why should we bother about her now?

There are many reasons why a twenty-first-century audience wanting to engage in philosophical reflection should read Wollstonecraft. The most commonly cited one is that she was an important precursor of feminist thought, and this is what I'm going to focus on particularly in this book. Her arguments, even now, challenge us to think beyond the basic demands of rights for women that still constitute the greater part of what we think of as feminism. They allow us to see how, despite progress being made, there is still much that needs doing before feminists can count themselves successful. But what makes her arguments so compelling is their philosophical quality. Her insights into the workings of the human mind – in particular reason, the passions, and the imagination – help us understand better how we should engage with each other and the world.[1] And they certainly contribute to her social and political thought, which includes her feminism. Wollstonecraft should also be read because, in an age of atheist enlightenment, she strove to provide a moral theory that was compatible with the religion she knew (Church of England) but allowed for much broader interpretations of Christianity and greater tolerance. In a context where Eurocentric feminism (or white feminism) finds it hard to recognize the feminist positions of Muslim women, this is a particularly powerful stance to hold. She should, again, be read because of her particular contribution to political thought, her arguments that there could be no progress without liberty from oppression for all, because slavery will 'degrade the master and the abject dependent'. Whether one reads her as a proponent of liberalism, as Virginia Sapiro (1992) did in her *Vindication of the Rights of Virtue*, or as a republican thinker, following the traditions of English seventeenth-century republicanism, but with a strong alignment with the thought of the French and American Revolutions, Wollstonecraft is a political philosopher to contend with, one who was unflinchingly egalitarian at a time when equality meant at most that middle-class white men could perhaps have a vote.[2] And she

---

[1] For a concise discussion of Wollstonecraft's philosophy of mind, see Reuter (2022).
[2] For discussions and analyses of Wollstonecraft's republican thought, see Halldenius (2015) and Coffee (2018).

should be read because her works influenced, directly and indirectly, later versions of feminism, in the United States and elsewhere. All these are excellent reasons why Wollstonecraft should be read today.

All the above are excellent reasons to read Wollstonecraft, but here I have chosen to focus on them through the lens of one aspect of her thought, namely: her pioneering feminist thought and its implications not only for women but also for families, work, education, and politics. Before I turn to an explanation of what I mean by calling Wollstonecraft a feminist and why I have chosen to focus on this, I want to offer a brief exposition of Wollstonecraft's life and work which will help situate her thought in the turbulent times in which she lived.

Life and Works

Mary Wollstonecraft was born on 27 April 1759 in London. Her childhood was relatively difficult. Despite being middle class her family was not well off. Her father, a gambler and an alcoholic, spent the family's capital and had to move them from one part of the country to another – to ever-shrinking houses – to avoid his debtors. As well as having to put up with a violent father and a mother who did not seem to care for any of her children but her older son, Wollstonecraft suffered from a lack of formal education. She only went to school for a year and a half, during an unusually extended stay in Beverly, Yorkshire. She was mostly self-taught, taking advantage of friends' libraries and discussing her reading with them.

Wollstonecraft left home at eighteen to earn a living and travel as a lady's companion. She remained in that position for a year or so, but found that the position of a servant did not suit her, and she was called to return home – now back in London – to care for her dying mother. There she became close friends with a young woman, Fanny Blood, who shared her love of books and philosophy. After her mother died, Wollstonecraft moved in with Fanny's family, which was even poorer than her own, and paid her way by helping Fanny's mother make bonnets and sew buttonholes on rich women's clothes. Soon afterwards, Wollstonecraft, her sisters – Everina and Eliza – and Fanny Blood opened a school for girls. The school was located in the village of Newington Green – in North London, the home of a group of

Rational Dissenters – in a house found and financed by Sarah Burgh, the widow of writer and philosopher James Burgh. The school lasted until Fanny moved to Portugal to get married, and shortly afterwards became pregnant, which caused her fragile health to deteriorate. She died in childbirth, and Wollstonecraft – who was visiting her – stayed on for some months to help care for the baby. The school, left in the hands of her inexperienced and unwilling sisters, failed. After her return, Wollstonecraft tried to cover some of their debts by working as a governess in Ireland. Again, she did not last in the position, finding that the governess was precariously poised between being a family member and a servant, a very uncomfortable position where she was expected to care for the children as if they her own, but answer to their parents as the hired help.

It was during her time as a school head teacher and as a governess that Wollstonecraft began to write. Her first books were a short volume entitled *Thoughts on the Education of Daughters* and a semi-autobiographical novel, *Mary*. *Thoughts* was inspired by her experience as a girl child who did not receive a systematic education, and by reading James Burgh's *Thoughts on Education*. James Burgh, whose widow had helped Wollstonecraft start the school – and who had also found the governess's position for her – had been one of the leading figures in Newington Green's dissenting Academy, that is, a place where Dissenters – excluded from Oxford and Cambridge because they would not swear allegiance to the Church of England – could study. Dissenting Academies were known for great tolerance and egalitarian values. And although the Dissenters were perhaps not quite feminists in the sense that Wollstonecraft would come to be – Burgh in his treatise says very little about the education of women, and none of it terribly satisfying – they certainly offered a nurturing environment for her own views to develop.

Another great influence on Wollstonecraft's thought and career from her time spent in the dissenting village was philosopher and economist Richard Price, the Newington Green minister. Not only did his sermons help Wollstonecraft clarify her philosophical and political thought but also it was he who introduced her to her publisher, Joseph Johnson. It was Price also who, indirectly, caused Wollstonecraft to write the book that first made her noticed by the public. Her *Vindication of the Rights of Men* was a response to Edmund Burke's *Reflections on the Revolution in France*, which itself was a direct and quite personal attack on Price, who had given and published a speech in which he defended the values of that revolution. Wollstonecraft was the first to publish a reply. Hers was closely followed by Thomas Paine's *The Rights of Man*. It was after a dinner party where Paine and Wollstonecraft argued – her future husband, Godwin, was also present, and was not impressed – that Johnson encouraged Wollstonecraft to write her second *Vindication, the Rights of Woman*.

Her connection to the dissenting London publisher Joseph Johnson was a critical factor in Wollstonecraft's career as a writer. When she came to him, penniless and homeless, after the failure of her school, he not only took her novel, *Mary*, for publication but also took her in until she could find rooms of her own, gave her a job as a reviewer for his journal, *The Analytical Review*, and suggested books that she might write that would fit her interests and the market.

In this way, Wollstonecraft became the 'first of a new genus', as she wrote to her sister Everina, that is, not the first woman to make a living out of writing, but the first to have a job as a 'staff writer' with a regular income from reviewing and a guaranteed publisher for what she wrote (Waters 2004, 416). Johnson was also responsible for Wollstonecraft's bout of war journalism, which culminated in her (unfinished) book *A Moral and Historical View of the French Revolution*. When Wollstonecraft decided to travel to Paris, to witness the revolution first-hand, Johnson paid her way in exchange for letters he might publish about her impressions.

In France, while researching the history of the early days of the revolution, and discussing its progress with some of its actors – Condorcet, Brissot, and Madame Roland – she found the time to fall in love, get pregnant, and give birth to a daughter, Fanny. Her lover, Gilbert Imlay, turned out to be unreliable and left the mother of his child to set up home with an opera singer in London. Wollstonecraft reacted by jumping off a bridge and Imlay – hoping to distract her from her suicidal intentions – sent her off on an errand to investigate the theft of a cargo of silver he was sending to America. This is how Wollstonecraft ended up traveling in Scandinavia, with a toddler, a French maid, and depression, interviewing ship's captains and lawyers to try to recover the stolen silver (she did not, but she found out that it had been stolen and by whom). The book she wrote then, *Letters from Denmark, Sweden and Norway*, led to her (re)introduction to her future husband, the philosopher William Godwin. They got married when Wollstonecraft found she was pregnant again. The two had a short time together, during which they sought to reinvent family life in a way that suited their careers and their principles. They lived apart (opposite each other), so as not to impose too domestic a rhythm on their writing lives, but they also shared the care of little Fanny. Wollstonecraft died of puerperal fever eleven days after giving birth to her second daughter, Mary (later Mary Shelley). She was thirty-eight. She left several unfinished books, including the novel *Maria, or the Wrongs of Woman*, a book of lessons written for her daughters, and a fragment of a plan for the second volume of the *Vindication of the Rights of Woman*.

Feminism and Women's Rights

I've mentioned that my focus in this volume would be Wollstonecraft's feminist thought. Before getting started I need to set right a couple of points: one methodological and one more substantial. The methodological point is about the use of the term 'feminism', which, at the time Wollstonecraft wrote, hadn't yet been coined. Is it right to call her a feminist? The second point is about the way in which she was a feminist, and in particular, whether we should look in her works for a defence of women's rights. Here I will explain briefly what I see as her position on human rights, and why I think it's more fruitful to focus on her discussions of how rights were denied to a portion of humanity, what the mechanisms for refusing to treat people, whether the poor, women, or the enslaved, as rights-holders involve and what their consequences are for future efforts to re-instate those rights.

So first, the methodological point. 'Le féminisme' – it was first coined in French by Charles Fourier in the first half of the nineteenth century – was popularized as a name for the defence of women's rights against patriarchal oppression by Hubertine Auclerc from 1882 in a column called 'Le Féminisme'.[3] Can we call Wollstonecraft a feminist given that she died before the term was coined? We certainly can, and I will. The principles Wollstonecraft fought for in her writings were similar enough to those Hubertine Auclerc revendicated a century later that it makes sense to use the same term to denote them. A good test of this rule would be to imagine what Wollstonecraft might have said if someone had presented her with the word and asked her to endorse it. Would she have distanced herself from the concept of feminism, in its simplest, purest form, as the defence of women's rights? Certainly not, if we go by the title of her best-known book. She might have disagreed with Auclerc's view that the right to vote was the central purpose of feminism – this only makes sense in a democratic context – and she might, although it is not certain, have disagreed with other feminist revendications, such as the right to divorce and the right to abortion. But feminists do disagree about these issues, and this doesn't make them any less feminists. There isn't a fully fleshed feminism that all true feminists embrace. As Virginie Despentes wrote in her 2022 novel *Cher Connard*, some feminists draw their feminism from Simone de Beauvoir, others from Valerie Solanas, and there is no unique brand of feminism, but only feminisms, all with their different flavours and preferred points of view. This includes movements that don't call themselves feminist, because they wanted to distance themselves from the main feminist ideology of their times, such as the womanists in the United States, who wanted their struggle to acknowledge that not all women were white. So when I call Wollstonecraft a feminist, I use the term loosely to denote any attempt at fighting for women's civil, political, social, or moral place – not necessarily for their rights, or even for equality, but for improvement or simply recognition of their oppression.

Another issue with labelling Wollstonecraft as a feminist is that it does label her. And labelling any woman philosopher a feminist has the result that she is no longer perceived as a philosopher, or at any rate not a philosopher who is likely to be of general interest. All her work is reduced to one particular problem, that of asserting the rights of the

---

[3] See Offen 1988, 45, on the origins of the word feminism and Eichner 2009 for Auclert's contribution to its dissemination.

female sex. That she was labelled a feminist, 'the mother of feminism', is part of the reason why, even after philosophers began to write about her, her books could only be found in the women or gender studies sections of bookshops, but never on the philosophy shelf. This was still true in 2013 when my *Routledge Guidebook to the Vindication of the Rights of Woman* came out, and I went to look for it in a London bookshop.[4]

Philosophers have done a great job of showing why Wollstonecraft was so much more than the 'mother of feminism', and why her works should be studied in philosophy classes as well as gender studies. The risks associated with labelling her as a feminist have hopefully dissipated, which means that now it's time to come back to her status as a precursor of feminism, and show how philosophers and everyone else should read her for that reason too.

One worry we might have about calling her a feminist is the way in which this might obscure her pioneering work on human rights. Wollstonecraft's defence of women's rights was, many thinkers have argued, a defence of women's human rights, and to cast her as a feminist may mean that we lose sight of that. I will argue that this is not the case, that although Wollstonecraft's account of women's human rights is central to her work, and that it frames her feminism, it is far from all there is to it. What Wollstonecraft offers that is truly distinctive, as a feminist, is a study of the mechanisms of oppression for those whose human rights are trampled and denied. And it is this aspect of her work that makes her so relevant to modern-day feminists who care about more than universal principles, but also, and perhaps more importantly, about uncovering the mechanisms of patriarchal oppression.

Wollstonecraft did attempt to develop and promote the concept of human rights, and when she argued for women's rights, it was for women's human rights. Her project was to get women recognized as full members of the human species, and therefore subject to the same rights as other human beings – men. But her discussion of rights is perhaps not as fully fleshed out as one might expect. Despite her having written two books advertised (in the title) as vindications of rights, there

---

[4] That same year, I visited Oxford and in Blackwell's asked where I might find a book by Wollstonecraft: I was directed to the travel literature section. Godwin was on the political philosophy shelf.

is not a page or a chapter where Wollstonecraft details her theory of human rights, or indeed offers a list of rights similar to the 1789 French *Rights of Man and Citizen*. Rights, for Wollstonecraft, are foundational and they are asserted more often than defended – especially in the *Vindication of the Rights of Men*, where they serve an important rhetorical purpose against Burke (Halldenius 2015, 44). Burke argues that aristocratic privileges should be preserved, because they secure the structure of society, even while they trample the most basic rights of the poor. Wollstonecraft counters that such societal structures probably should not be preserved.

It is perhaps because their role is foundational and rhetorical that Wollstonecraft does not expand on the list of rights she regards as essential: the right to equality, the right to liberty or independence, and the right to 'friendship' (Lefebvre 2019, 436). It is possible that Wollstonecraft intended to codify rights in a later volume. She mentions in the advertisement of the *Vindication of the Rights of Woman* that she intends the second volume to discuss the laws relating to women and their peculiar duties (Wollstonecraft 2014, 25). That volume remained unwritten, but we can perhaps look to contemporary texts such as Olympe de Gouges's *Declaration of the Rights of Woman* to get an idea of what such a list of rights might have looked like.

Just as the French declaration of rights prefaced, and perhaps called for, the revolution, Wollstonecraft claims that recognizing women's human rights must be the condition of what she calls a 'revolution in female manners'. Women do not, she believes, behave as citizens should because they have been brought up to behave as less than human. In order to bring about change in their behaviour, we must first convince them – and their male companions – that they are in fact fully human. Once that has happened, the necessary revolution can take place:

> It is time to effect a revolution in female manners – time to restore to them their lost dignity – and make them, as a part of the human species, labour by reforming themselves to reform the world. (Wollstonecraft 2014, 71; see also 210 and 214)

The reason why rights are foundational for Wollstonecraft, and why they are crucial to her proposal for a revolution in female manners, is that they are the logical condition for our having any duties towards each other (Halldenius 2015, 35). If women have no rights, then they have no duties to behave one way or the other, and one should be grateful that they are following some rules of behaviour at all – rules imposed by their husbands, and not requiring the use of reason. But if we want them to own their existence and be accountable for the way they act, we must first grant them rights. No real discussion of women's 'manners' or virtue can happen if we do not first grant that women have rights.

How are duties and rights connected for Wollstonecraft? She believes that women's rights are human rights, that is, they are the rights that all human beings share, by virtue of being rational and capable of understanding moral right and wrong. It is *qua* human and rational beings that we have rights. It is in virtue of our humanity that we are owed respect. In that, Wollstonecraft does not differ a great deal from Kant when he argues that human beings are ends in themselves because they are rational and that to act in a way that is morally right requires that we recognize and respect this (Kant 2012, 4: 428–9; Botting 2016, 31). The ability to create moral principles and to want to obey them is what is distinctive of humanity, and what is inherently worthy of respect. It is also, therefore, because we are human beings capable of moral reasoning that that we have duties: rights and duties are inseparably bound to our nature.

A challenge that Wollstonecraft and other eighteenth-century feminists like Olympe de Gouges had to meet was to convince the world to recognize women's humanity, and as a result start seeing the rights that were naturally theirs. This was a challenge because when men do not recognize women's humanities, they are in a position to exercise power over them, and to disregard any protest they make. Just as a master will train his dog in whichever way suits him best, and judge the dog's behaviour according to the dog's ability to perform and follow orders, husbands and fathers like to take it upon themselves to shape their wives and daughters in whichever way suits them best. Rousseau, whose work was read and admired by men and women throughout Europe, in his bestselling *Emile ou de l'Education* recommended that girls' main quality be docility, which will make it easier to live subjected to the will of imperfect men, and he asked that mothers be complicit in preparing their daughters to be flexible servants for their future husbands, as this is the role that fits their nature best (Rousseau 1979, 368). To go counter to Rousseau and argue that women's manners ought to be determined by what they had in common with men, not their supposed difference, was definitely an uphill struggle.

But, as Wollstonecraft saw, the challenge itself contains a strategy for defeating the idea that women are somehow not as human as men: if they have no rights because they are not fully human or rational, then they can have no duties either. This becomes obvious once we look more closely at the idea that women are to be trained, like animals, by men, their masters. A big part of Wollstonecraft's argument for women's human rights is to point out that this strategy – of treating women as animals that must be trained to suit their master's needs or desires – is bound to failure. Women, she observes, are expected to do more than perform the simple tricks and services that dogs are trained to do. They are expected to be virtuous in their relations to their husband, their children, and anyone else they come across. But virtue is not something that can be impressed on an animal with a whip. A dog that is told not to touch food on the table will probably disobey if no one is looking. It feels no moral compunction to obey – regardless of whether the dog is capable of moral sentiment. Having been trained with a whip or a rolled-up newspaper to avoid behaving in certain ways is not the same as having been taught that it is wrong to do so.

A mother is expected to care for her children even when no one is looking. Not only that, she is also expected to teach them how to be virtuous – and that she cannot do if she has no understanding of virtue herself: all she can do is teach them to avoid the sort of behaviour that will get them – or her – into trouble, modelling her teaching on her own experience. But while this may be considered sufficient for a girl child, it won't do for a boy, who needs to grow to become a rights-holder and a trainer of women. So, women, if they are not virtuous themselves, should be completely segregated from their sons.

The claim that women are either rational and should be treated as human beings, with the same rights men have in virtue of their humanity, or they are animals and should not be expected to perform any human duties is discussed at the beginning and at the end of the second *Vindication*. In the Introduction, Wollstonecraft writes that women 'are treated as a kind of subordinate beings, and not as part of the human species, when improveable reason is allowed to be the dignified distinction which raises men above the brute creation' (Wollstonecraft 2014, 30). In Chapter 2, she enjoins men to make up their minds whether women are human beings, like them, or animals. And if the latter, she says:

> [S]hould it then appear, that like the brutes they were principally created for the use of man, he will let them patiently bite the bridle, and not mock them with empty praise; or, should their rationality be proved, he will not impede their improvement merely to gratify his sensual appetites. (Wollstonecraft 2014, 61)

If women are not rational, Wollstonecraft says, they should be treated with kindness, but they should not be required to perform above their capacities, and they should be held to standards of morality that are only accessible to rational beings. On the very final page of the *Vindication of the Rights of Woman*, Wollstonecraft reiterates this point, backing it more explicitly with the principle that duties cannot be separated from rights:

> Let woman share the rights and she will emulate the virtues of man; for she must grow more perfect when emancipated, or *justify the authority that chains such a weak being to her duty.* – If the latter, it will be expedient to open a fresh trade with Russia for whips; a present which a father should always make to his son-in-law on his wedding day, that a husband may keep his whole family in order by the same means; and without any violation of justice reign, wielding this sceptre, sole master of his house, *because he is the only being in it who has reason*: – the divine, indefeasible earthly sovereignty breathed into man by the Master of the universe. Allowing this position, women have not any inherent rights to claim; and, by the same rule, their duties vanish, *for rights and duties are inseparable*. (Wollstonecraft 2014, 226 my emphases)

If women are denied reason, she goes on, they must be allowed 'the privileges of ignorance', and men who would expect virtue from them would be most unreasonable. In this way, the argument that women are also human rights-holders frames the second *Vindication*: if they are human, they are rational, and if they are rational, they have rights. But if they have no rights, they can have no duties. Given that women are expected to develop virtues and act dutifully, they must be human.

Therefore, their human status and human rights must be recognized before their virtues can be improved through education.

Elsewhere in the book Wollstonecraft shows how granting, respecting, or trampling on these rights affects the progress of human society, and in particular, how a partial offering of human rights (to men, or to rich and white men) cannot have the desired result of creating a better-functioning human society that improves upon the virtue and happiness of existing societies. Only if human rights are granted to all humans, she argues, echoing the rallying cry of French Revolutionary men – but, unlike them, meaning it – will they make the difference that is hoped for. So while the *Vindications* are very much about rights, as their titles suggest, they, and especially the second *Vindication*, are about rights in a particular way. This way invites us to study the effects of denying rights to a portion of the population, whether because they are poor, or female, or black, and how the overall effect of withholding rights is the hampering of human progress, and therefore bad for all. In doing this, and in particular in her review of women's situations, Wollstonecraft encourages us to study the background values and prejudices that prevent women from enjoying their rights.

Many of the prejudices Wollstonecraft uncovers are specific to a culture, a society, a time. But a lot of them are also enduring. One she stresses particularly is dress codes for women, which privileges beauty and attractiveness over health (Wollstonecraft 2014, 68, 113, 199). The dictates of women's dress meant that women could not exercise, even if they'd wanted to, and this resulted in poor health and lack of physical strength. Although one might be tempted to say that this is much less of an issue than it was in the eighteenth century, because we no longer wear corsets, for instance, and because for many women it's perfectly acceptable to go out wearing yoga pants, hoodies, and trainers, it would be a mistake to think that the problem has disappeared. A recent study of the prevalence of allergies and respiratory diseases in North America traced a disparity between men and women sufferers to the clothes boys and girls wear at kindergarten. Feminist philosopher of science Sharyn Clough (2011) noted that the fact that women tended to be more prone to respiratory diseases, which was caused by a lower exposure to microorganisms that would help build immunity in childhood, could be linked to the fact that 'girls are dressed more often than boys in clothing that is not supposed to get dirty' (Clough 2011, 413).

Still, the eighteenth-century etiquette and rules that are decried in Wollstonecraft's work are not always easy to relate to outside of their very specific context. They are very much descriptive of late eighteenth-century European ways of living (mostly in England, but at times in France, Portugal, and Scandinavia), and sifting through these descriptions may sound like too much work for a feminist who is not also a historian. More importantly, perhaps, it may seem as though Wollstonecraft cared exclusively about a very particular set of oppressions which applied to women of her constituency, that is, white, middle class, and European.

How is reading about these women and their very specific oppression useful for a generation of feminists who seek to move away from the particular and somewhat privileged oppression of the white middle-class cishet northern European woman? Why add to that particularity 'living in the eighteenth century'? One reason why Wollstonecraft's careful study of the cultural and social context for the oppression of women is useful for us, who do not share that culture or society, is that it shows us how oppression is best understood with reference to this sort of detail, rather than from a purely universalist perspective. Feminists such as Serene Khader and Rafia Zakaria have warned us against relying entirely on universal principles if we want to fight oppression for all women, and not just those like us.[5] This may sound counterintuitive – after all, universalism is about going beyond one's own situation and finding what is common to all. But Khader and others have pointed out that the white feminist conception of universalism may not be as universalist as they think. Attempting to derive universal principles from the narrow perspective of women who tend to lead similar lives and face similar problems carries the risk that we make generalizations that apply only to this sort of women and fail to be at all universal. Better instead to focus on what is particular about each type of oppression, and that requires looking at the prejudices that are attached to local and time-specific women's lives. Wollstonecraft's decoding of what she calls 'manners' is for this reason extremely valuable. It shows us what kind of work

---

[5] See Khader (2017) and Zakaria (2021).

intersectional and decolonial feminists might do to understand the real spread of women's oppression, as it focuses us on finding the deeply embedded social particularities that make it so difficult to uproot.

This brings us back to the question of the place of women's human rights in Wollstonecraft's discourse. Wollstonecraft needed her audience to recognize that women were as much a part of humanity as men. But would she have been satisfied if all that was achieved was that women were considered as humans? She might have been very satisfied if she could be confident that she had achieved this. But there was a lot more to her programme. Wollstonecraft understood that in being deprived of their rights, women had lost more than a valuable status in society. The denying of their rights had chipped away at their humanity and their capacity to enjoy their rights once they were returned to them. Women had become 'convenient slaves' and did not perceive themselves as human rights holders, 'as slavery will have its constant effect, degrading the master and abject dependent' (Wollstonecraft 2014, 23). For this reason, not only men but also women guarded the gates of patriarchy, and prevented women from joining the ranks of human subjects. What needed to be done, then, was to persuade men, but especially women, that they were human rights-holders, that they were not by nature subservient to men, and that it was wrong to hold them in that position – morally wrong, but also bad for them, for the men who kept them so, and for any children they had together.

The above argument is why Wollstonecraft's project for women's rights is first and foremost an educational project: men and women need to understand what human rights are, how they are the reflection of human nature (itself mirroring divine nature), and how all members of the species are capable of being guided by reason and virtue. Recognizing that these are universal and essential human traits makes it much harder to deny women's humanity. If your wives are not rational, Wollstonecraft told husbands (in the two passages quoted earlier), then they are not human. If they are not human, they are animals. And if they are animals, are they fit to share your bed and raise your children? But again, the educational project is not sufficient: simply writing books telling people that women are humans too, while important, will not suffice to bring about large-scale change. What is needed, Wollstonecraft argues, is a *revolution in female manners*. Manners, which are taught but not codified, which are regarded as proper, but never deduced from moral principles, are part of the fabric of society. It is this very fabric that we must study and deconstruct, Wollstonecraft says, in order to help women realize their full humanity. And deconstructing the fabric of society is revolutionary – as Burke argued, to reject manners it is to break through the veil that holds everything and everyone together, and keeps them in their proper place (Burke 1986, 171). Wollstonecraft is all for tearing down that veil and making revolutionary cockades with it.

Outline of the Book

The first point to investigate is whether Wollstonecraft's feminism really is relevant to the concerns of today's feminists. In Chapter 2, we look at some objections to my claim that it is, and I defend that claim further, showing that Wollstonecraft can be considered a precursor of decolonial and intersectional feminism. What did she have to say about class, slavery and racism, and gender and sexual orientation?

Wollstonecraft urges women to break their chains and claim the civil existence (and thus rights) that should be theirs. But, rather than simply haranguing them, or telling them 'wake up' and claim their rights, as Olympe de Gouges did, she was greatly concerned with what stopped them from doing that. Why did women not rise against their oppressors, why did they remain 'abject slaves' for such a long time? The study of what stops the oppressed from revolting is central to Wollstonecraft's feminist philosophy and key to understanding almost everything else. For this reason, this will be the subject of Chapter 3. In Chapter 4, we will turn to one particular focus of Wollstonecraft's views on oppression and liberation: the body. Women, she argues, are stunted in their upbringing, not just in their ability to pursue knowledge and virtue but also in their physical strength and health. Poor health leads to weakness, which reinforces women's dependence on men. And conversely, men's unhealthy lifestyle (Wollstonecraft spends a great deal of time talking about syphilis) further weakens women. The body also plays an important role in Wollstonecraft's views on the maternal body, so we will spend some time on this, including on abortion.

Wollstonecraft wrote a great deal about the education of children: one short treatise, *Thoughts on the Education of Daughters*, a book for children and educators, *Original Stories for Children*, and an unfinished primer she wrote for her daughter. In all these, and in relevant sections of the *Rights of Woman*, she argued that children should be taught to use their reason, to feel appropriate emotions, and to respect each other. All of this has a strong relational element: Wollstonecraft suggests that adults should encourage children to ask questions, and leave children to argue amongst themselves, so as to use their reason more freely. Her notion of parental responsibility and childhood duties, underlying her educational programme, turns out to be just as radical as her other ideas. Wollstonecraft equates the responsibilities of mothers and fathers, and argues against the (then predominant) view of parents as having the right to do as they chose with their children, proposing some limitations to parental domination. This will be the focus of Chapter 5.

While Wollstonecraft partly ascribes women's inability or unwillingness to rise against their oppressor to perceived physical and intellectual weakness – how will I cope in the world without my husband to provide and tell me what to do? – she also puts strong emphasis on the power of work to provide strength and independence. Working-class women, for instance, know that they can make their own way in the world without men to support them. Chapter 6 focuses on the place of work and experience of the world in Wollstonecraft's moral and political philosophy, and in particular her feminist thought, as she argues that one way in which women are held back is by not being allowed to investigate the world and move freely in the public space. She sometimes blames early marriage, as it simply removes a young woman from her parent's home to that of her husband, who will himself have left home as a child to go to school, later possibly to travel, and still leaves most days to go to work. Women, Wollstonecraft argues both in *Thoughts on the Education of Daughters* and in *A Vindication of the Rights of Woman*, should pursue their development outside the home, either by leading professional lives or by pursuing intellectual or artistic interests once their children are old enough to go to school. There can be no independence for women, Wollstonecraft argues, without work that goes beyond domestic work.

In Chapter 7, we look at how Wollstonecraft's political thought was shaped by her study of oppression, but also by the political activism around her – in particular the French Revolution – and how she helped shape the new social and political frameworks that were developing at the time. Her commentaries on the French Revolution, in her *Moral and Historical View of the French Revolution*, and on Scandinavian societies, in her *Letters from Denmark, Sweden and Norway*, help us understand how engaged a thinker she was, and how she committed to the improvement of social and political conditions for all. Is Wollstonecraft's intention to improve life conditions for all, or only for the oppressed? What about those who are on the side of the oppressors, that is, rich white men? Finally, Chapter 8 explores the place of men and masculinity in Wollstonecraft's thought, and the new world she hoped would rise. Unlike Charlotte Perkins Gilman, she never envisaged a world without men, but always hoped that men and women could learn to live and work together. In order for this to happen, social mores needed to be reformed, as they contained too many prejudices about sex and gender that kept men and women separate. How close have we come to realizing Wollstonecraft's vision? Perhaps not close enough, but we are at least trying. One reason why we should all be reading Wollstonecraft now is that she will help us ask the questions that need to be asked in order to make progress on a more inclusive, more progressive, and fairer world.

CHAPTER 2

Standing Up for All the Oppressed

George Eliot, when she reviewed Wollstonecraft's *Vindication of the Rights of Woman*, found it 'eminently serious, severely moral, and withal rather heavy' (Eliot 1855). First-wave feminist Emma Goldman possibly agreed, as she looked to Wollstonecraft's life, rather than her works, for inspiration. Then, second-wave feminists thought her too prim and bourgeois to bother with at all. For a long time after her death Wollstonecraft's books were confined to the basements of antiquarian bookshops, and rarely got a mention in philosophical publications. Not until quite recently was she taken seriously again as a philosopher and a feminist.

Should we take our cue from previous generations of feminists and look elsewhere for philosophical inspiration? After all, there might be good historical (and feminist) reasons for reading Wollstonecraft that have nothing to do with how she can be of use to us in thinking through modern dilemmas. Still today, many (analytic) philosophers believe, for instance, that Descartes was utterly wrong about most things, but this doesn't mean that they recommend we leave him out of our syllabi. Reading Descartes, at the very least, provides the necessary background for understanding the course that the history of metaphysics and epistemology took. Reading Wollstonecraft may help us understand the history of feminist thought and more. But I want to argue that we have more urgent reasons to read her, that is, that Wollstonecraft far from being a 'bourgeois' feminist was in fact a precursor of intersectional feminism. Throughout her writings Wollstonecraft demonstrates a deep concern for women who are poor, enslaved, as well as those whose lives are limited by prejudice and social institutions. Her last, unfinished text, *Maria or the Wrongs of Women*, offers a striking account of how poverty acts on a woman's capacity for freedom. And her two *Vindications*, along with the book reviews she wrote for *The Analytical Review*, show a keen engagement with the abolitionist movements in England and France.

The Unperishable Heart: Or Why Wollstonecraft Was Nearly Erased

> It appears to me impossible that I should cease to exist, or that this active, restless spirit, equally alive to joy and sorrow, should only be organised dust – ready to fly abroad the moment the spring snaps, or the spark goes out which kept it together. Surely something resides in this heart that is not perishable, and life is more than a dream.
> *Letters from Sweden.* 1796 (Wollstonecraft 1989, Vol 5, 281)

Mary Wollstonecraft was rowing across the Norwegian sea looking for a spot where she could swim when she was struck by this bout of optimism. Things could go well, for her, now and forever. She was not insignificant, and she was persistent: her spirit would carry on after her death. While we can't comment as to whether her spirit did persist in a religious sense, we can confirm that she was right, and that her life's work, motivated always by that spirit, still moves the minds and hearts of many who come across it, one way or another. The problem is that until recently not that many people did.

I first came across Mary Wollstonecraft a mere fifteen years ago, when I read her *Vindications of the Rights of Woman* for a course I was teaching. Very soon afterwards I met other scholars who worked on Wollstonecraft, and we formed lasting friendships based on our enthusiasm for her work. Together we worked on recovering it and making it more accessible to our colleagues, students, and the general public. Wollstonecraft was not easy to find, back then, unless you were looking in the 'women's studies' section of an academic bookshop. But the more people rediscovered her work, the more they talked about it, the more accessible it became. Of course, we are not talking of a mass recognition of Wollstonecraft's work. Roberta Wedge – who offers Wollstonecraft tours of London – once joked that ten years ago if we'd asked people in the streets of London where Wollstonecraft lived and worked, what the name Wollstonecraft meant to them, only 1 in 100 would have known we were talking about a woman author. Now, she says, 2 in 100 would respond! That seems disheartening, but how many women philosophers have members of the public heard of? As a matter of fact, would they recognize male philosophers of the past? Leibniz? Malebranche? Possibly not. So 2 in 100 would in fact be a good result.

Mary Wollstonecraft – despite her contributions to moral and political philosophy, to aesthetics, and to literature in general – did get swallowed up by the general forgetfulness that attaches itself to women authors, but thanks to the movement for the recovery of these same authors, she is now very close to taking up her place and legacy, in philosophy and elsewhere, in universities and the streets. A legitimate question is why this hasn't happened earlier. In her now seminal paper, Eileen O'Neill (1997, 20) named the problem of finding women's works in philosophy curricula 'disappearing ink'. Philosophers who were published, read, and discussed during their lifetimes are no longer published, read, or discussed. Their printed words have disappeared. The reasons are varied: sometimes women's work fails to capture the interest of those who might reprint it or comment on it – because it is written by women – or discusses women and is therefore not considered of universal interest. In the case of Mary Wollstonecraft, all this is true. But there is also the fact that her husband's biography of her – published weeks after her death – revealed many intimate details of her life, including her relationship with Henri Fuseli, who was married at the time, her becoming a mother out of wedlock, and her two suicide attempts. These were distinctly not what one would expect of a respectable British woman. This meant that her popularity as an author fell after her death, and that, in part, is the reason why her works were not reprinted or discussed. Her works were shelved and forgotten.[1] Those who did read her, as John Stuart Mill and Harriet Taylor no doubt did, were discreet about it. There are no references to her works in *The Subjection of Women* or Taylor's 'The Enfranchisement

---

[1] At least in Britain; translations of her works in French were still being reviewed by Pierre Roederer: *Maria* in 1798 and *Marie et Caroline* (*Original Stories*) in 1799.

of Women', published in 1851 in *The Westminster Review*, even while her influence is clearly visible.

Finally, while one might have expected a renewed interest in Wollstonecraft once feminists were beginning to organize and to look back to texts that supported their causes, this did not happen.[2] Wollstonecraft was, to a large extent, shunned by her natural allies. When Virginia Woolf or Emma Goldman wrote about Wollstonecraft, it was her life, rather than her works, they liked to discuss. They saw her as a free spirit, treating with contempt the social institutions and rules that kept women down. They saw her as a woman struggling to become accepted for her writings – in a world that only valued women's work when it was conducted in the obscurity of the home – and for the good of the men. Her life – or the legend of her life transmitted by her widower William Godwin – was perhaps more exciting and relatable than her works, which were altogether very serious, dealing with topics such as human rights and virtue, and discussing in detail the works of contemporary authors such as Edmund Burke or Richard Price, which perhaps made them seem cumbersome or irrelevant to readers concerned with more immediate problems.

The advent of second-wave feminism meant that once again the life of Wollstonecraft was rediscovered and that it was held up as an exemplar of resistance by feminists who read about her childhood attempts at protecting her mother from her violent father (Murray 2020, 61). Unfortunately, the works themselves did not hold up to scrutiny with second-wave feminists. They thought Wollstonecraft not radical enough, because she still saw motherhood as essentially a woman's work (Ford 2009, 190). And they thought her too 'bourgeois' because she wrote primarily for white middle-class women (Myers 1988, 206).

More recently, Wollstonecraft has been held up to the standards of intersectional feminism.[3] Given that she does talk about race, in the context of transatlantic slavery, and more generally cultural and religious differences – she talks about 'eastern women' – do her arguments

---

[2] Here I use 'feminists' loosely to refer to anyone who argued or acted on behalf of the betterment of women's conditions. See my comment in the introductory chapter.
[3] See Vergès 2021, discussed later in this chapter.

demonstrate the kind of racism we should be wary of? And finally, while she has been criticized (again by second-wave feminists) as a sexual prude, can anything she writes about women be applied to a more comprehensive understanding of genders and sexual orientations? Very few early modern philosophers do stand up to scrutiny when it comes to such questions. Yet they remain on our bookshelves, having established their philosophical excellence before the questioning began. Can someone like Wollstonecraft, who is not as well established, continue to fight their way into our curricula and research while the intersectional challenge is going on? This is what I'll try to answer in the following sections.

'The Most Natural State' – Wollstonecraft on Social Class

It is no mystery why Wollstonecraft is so often branded a bourgeois philosopher: in her most read book *The Vindication of the Rights of Woman*, she argues that reform must happen first in the middle classes, because they are the most ready for it, they are her natural constituency, they are her readers, and they are the women who are in a position to act on her words:

> [A]ddressing my sex in a firmer tone, I pay particular attention to those in the middle class, because they appear to be in the most natural state. Perhaps the seeds of false-refinement, immorality, and vanity, have ever been shed by the great. Weak, artificial beings, raised above the common wants and affections of their race, in a premature unnatural manner, undermine the very foundation of virtue and spread corruption through the whole mass of society! (Wollstonecraft 2014, 31)

But Wollstonecraft is not defending the rights of middle-class women at the expense of everyone else. What she believes is that the middle classes are a better target for improvement than the aristocrats, because they are not corrupted in the same way. Aristocratic women are too far gone into moral decay to be in a realistic position to reclaim and regain any of their lost independence. But what about the poorer classes who were omnipresent in late eighteenth-century London? Is Wollstonecraft simply not interested in helping women who live in poverty? This is certainly not something we can deduce from the passage quoted. Wollstonecraft is addressing her readers, and – having worked for the publisher Joseph Johnson for several years at the time she wrote the *Vindication* – she knows that the poor of England do not form a significant part of her readership. If she is to produce social and political change through her writing, then she has to act on her readers first. And there is little point in asking women with no civil existence of their own to battle for the social and political rights of women poorer than them. Best, she thinks, to start the revolution with those who can act, and then let it spread.

It is also not clear that Wollstonecraft believes working-class women are oppressed in quite the same way middle-class women are. They are oppressed by poverty. But their oppression is much closer to that of their husbands, brothers, and sons than it is to their middle-class sisters. They are not ornaments or birds in gilded cages, singing for luxury. Free from this luxury, they are more likely to be uncorrupted:

> Happy is it when people have the cares of life to struggle with; for these struggles prevent their becoming a prey to enervating vices, merely from idleness! (Wollstonecraft 2014, 82)

This seems rather cold and insensitive: poor people should be happy that they are poor as they will not become corrupted! But there is also a more positive turn in Wollstonecraft's take on lower-class women: not only are they not corrupted by luxury but also this is visible in their comportment:

> With respect to virtue, to use the word in a comprehensive sense, I have seen most in low life. Many poor women maintain their children by the sweat of their brow, and keep together families that the vices of the fathers would have scattered abroad; but gentlewomen are too indolent to be actively virtuous, and are softened rather than refined by civilization. Indeed, the good sense which I have met with, among the poor women who have had few advantages of education, and yet have acted heroically, strongly confirmed me in the opinion that trifling employments have rendered woman a trifler. (Wollstonecraft 2014, 104)

This first-hand experience she mentions is almost certainly related to her time spent living with Fanny Blood's family, before she founded the school at Newington Green. Fanny's mother was a seamstress and had to work late into the night, by weak candlelight, in order to make sufficient money to feed her family.

The Vindication of the Rights of Woman professes to address itself to middle-class women, because they are in a better position to bring about change for themselves and others, but also because they are in need of change that they only can bring about by exercising 'power over themselves', that is, rejecting the trade offered them of luxury for truth and liberty. Upper-class women are

> treated like queens only to be deluded by hollow respect, till they are led to resign, or not assume, their natural prerogatives? Confined then in cages like the feathered race, they have nothing to do but to plume themselves, and stalk with mock majesty from perch to perch. It is true they are provided with food and raiment, for which they neither toil nor spin; but health, liberty, and virtue, are given in exchange. (Wollstonecraft 2014, 83)

Working-class women certainly do not need to be told to leave the luxury of home and contribute to society through their work: they are already doing that. What they do need is better pay and work conditions, recognition of the value of the work they do, and protection from the violence of men who would exploit them with impunity because they are poor. In any case, Wollstonecraft is not prone to either romanticizing or vilifying the poor. When Edmund Burke, in his eagerness to show that the French Revolution was an all-round evil, described the women who marched down to Versailles as 'furies of hell, in the abused shape of the vilest of women', Wollstonecraft replied, matter-of-factly: 'Probably you mean women who gained a livelihood by selling vegetables or fish, who never had had any advantages of education' (1989 vol. 5, 30). Poverty, to her, is not a mark of character but simply a social and economic disadvantage which prevents some from developing in the way they ought, but also keeps them safe from certain corruptions that only touch the very rich.

Wollstonecraft is very clear on the differences between oppression for women in different social classes – her final (unfinished) work, *Maria or the Wrongs of Women*, discusses just that. In the novel she sets up two exploited and abused women: one aristocratic, Maria, and the other working class, Jemima. Maria is imprisoned in an asylum for the insane by her abusive husband who wants control over her money. She is separated from her baby and has no friend she can appeal to for help.

Jemima – the illegitimate child of a servant, abused as a teenager, then prostituted – managed to educate herself sufficiently to get a job as a jailor in the asylum where Maria is kept. The two women's woes are set beside each other, and the reader sees that although there are striking differences due to their classes (Maria always had food and a comfortable roof over her head, even when that roof was a prison, while Jemima was forced at times to live in the streets, and sell her body to survive), there are also similarities in their troubles. Both are at the mercy of men who control their bodies and their minds, but also can take their children away from them. Neither can live an independent life, or be free to care for those they love. If the *Vindication of the Rights of Woman* is a manual for a revolution in manners to be started by middle-class women, *Maria* shows those middle-class readers that the sufferings of women from all classes are very real, and that while aristocratic women are just as dependent on the goodwill of men for their well-being and freedom, working-class women also have to contend with abject poverty, which makes them, and sometimes their abusers, less visible than richer women, and less likely to have their cause championed. By making it more visible, it is clear that Wollstonecraft is trying to become that champion, and encourage those she rallied to her cause when she wrote the *Vindication* to include working-class women in their fight for justice.

Wollstonecraft was briefly installed on the feminist bandwagons of the seventies, but was then thrown out again mainly because people had read only her *Vindication of the Rights of Woman* and had found it wanting in terms of class awareness and radicalism. It seemed as though Wollstonecraft was not doing much beyond asking that women should be educated so that they could perform their subservient domestic roles more efficiently. A look at some of her other texts – *A Vindication of the Rights of Men*, where she defends the French Revolution, or *Maria*, where she exposes the wrongs that working-class as well as upper-class women are subjected to because of their sex – would have brought her back to one of the front seats.

Second-wave feminists, when they rejected Wollstonecraft as too 'bourgeois', failed to see that Wollstonecraft's work had the potential for being far more inclusive than even they were. They saw Wollstonecraft as a middle-class woman fighting for some recognition for her kind, that is, other white, British, middle-class women. They did not see that her fight extended beyond her class, her sex or gender, her nationality, and even her race. To be fair, none of this was terribly clear from a cursory reading of her *Vindication of the Rights of Woman*, which is presumably all that a feminist activist of the second wave would have had time for. This more inclusive interpretation of Wollstonecraft's work requires context, that is, reading other books she wrote, and understanding the ideas and events she was responding to as she wrote them. But now that this work has been done – by many scholars over the last thirty years – there is really no excuse. We can and should ask what sort of feminist Wollstonecraft was, and whether we owe her a place on our bookshelves as the major social and political philosopher she was, a champion of human rights and freedom for all.

'Like the Poor African Slaves': Wollstonecraft on Race and Slavery

In a recent book on what decolonial and intersectional feminism should look like, Françoise Vergès criticized eighteenth-century women philosophers for appropriating the language of slavery in order to argue for women's rights:

> By drawing an analogy between their situation and that of slaves, European feminists denounced a position of dependence, a status of minors-for-life. But in doing so they erased the central elements of slavery – capture, deportation, sale, trafficking, torture, denial of social and family ties, rape, exhaustion, racism, sexism, and death that framed the lives of female slaves appropriating through analogy a condition that was not theirs. (Vergès 2021, 28)

Vergès adds that even feminist authors from that period who looked at slavery directly tended to romanticize it, and expected the enslaved to be submissive and patient, while the white heroes or heroines saved them. She takes Olympe de Gouges as an example. Gouges was one of the few eighteenth-century authors to defend abolitionism entirely, without any reservation, or any requirement that the enslaved be educated first. Despite this, she did not escape certain racist prejudices, such as that the enslaved should be more patient and less violent than their white oppressors. She also poised herself as the enslaved's white saviour, and felt she could berate them when – by taking their fate into their own hands and staging violent upheavals – they failed to live up to her conceptions of what a good enslaved person should be like.

Olympe de Gouges is a poster child for how difficult it is – even for the well-intentioned – to really understand what slavery is, and address its victims without positioning oneself as superior in some way. Gouges was a prolific writer and she openly argued for the abolition of slavery in two plays and several pamphlets and open letters.[4] Wollstonecraft, although she touched on the topic in several texts, did not make the question of slavery central to any of her books. Just how deep did her defence of abolition go? Wollstonecraft was one of the eighteenth-century writers who used the analogy between women and slavery Vergès refers to. Moira Ferguson, in her 'Wollstonecraft and the Problematic of Slavery', notes that while in the *Vindication of the Rights of Men* there are only five references to slavery, in the *Rights of Woman* there are eighty. She adds, 'the constituency Wollstonecraft champions – white, middle-class women – is constantly characterized as slaves. For her major polemic, that is, Mary Wollstonecraft decided to adopt and adapt the terms of contemporary political debate' (Ferguson 1992, 82). This sounds almost as though Wollstonecraft is jumping on the abolitionist bandwagon, appropriating its vocabulary and arguments in order to push her own agenda – that of the emancipation of white middle-class British women. This is not at all what Ferguson is saying – she argues that Wollstonecraft was part of the abolitionist movement and that her references to it in the *Rights of Woman* are intended to strengthen arguments against slavery, rather than appropriate them and erase their original target.

Even before she wrote the *Vindication of the Rights of Woman*, Wollstonecraft's references to the practice of slavery in the Americas show that she did not seek to either diminish the plight of the enslaved or assimilate it to that of white middle-class women in England. In fact, it is clear that she sees white women as full participants in the practice of slavery. In the *Rights of Men*, she shows off Burke's characterization of

---

[4] For a discussion of Gouges's abolitionist work, see my 2022a. For a discussion of eighteenth-century French abolitionist debate, see my 2022b.

aristocratic women as virtuous and decorous by referring to the well-documented cruelty of white women in plantations:

> Where is the dignity, the infallibility of sensibility, in the fair ladies, whom, if the voice of rumour is to be credited, the captive negroes curse in all the agony of bodily pain, for the unheard of tortures they invent? It is probable that some of them, after the sight of a flagellation, compose their ruffled spirits and exercise their tender feelings by the perusal of the last imported novel.–How true these tears are to nature, I leave you to determine. (1989, vol 5, 45)

Abolitionism was an important part of Wollstonecraft's circle's concerns. The rational dissenters, like the members of the Clapham sect, were activists as well as intellectuals. They sought to help the oppressed all over the world and helped circulate the testimonies of individuals who had been enslaved and wrote about it, such as Ottobah Coguano and Olaudah Equiano. The abolitionist movement itself was developing and the Abolition Committee was formed in May 1787. Moira Ferguson links the founding of Johnson and Christie's *Analytical Review* (to which Wollstonecraft contributed until her death) to the growing abolitionist movement, and notes that Wollstonecraft's early reviews reflected that concern (Ferguson 1992, 83–4).

Olaudah Equiano, a writer and activist who was born into slavery, spoke at the Unitarian church at Newington Green at a time when Wollstonecraft attended sermons there. His book, published in 1789, *Interesting Narrative of the Life of Olaudah Equiano, or Gustavus Vassa, the African* was reviewed by Johnson's *Analytical Review* in May of that year, and at least in some accounts, Wollstonecraft was the reviewer.[5] Although she found the chapters on his religious faith rather dull (she writes that 'the narrative should have closed when he became his own master'), she was more enthusiastic about his account of his 'endeavours to obtain his freedom', which appealed to many of the same neo-republican principles she herself deployed in her writing.

---

[5] See Bugg, 2006, Donington, 2020, 226 and also Hunt Botting (2021, 1310): 'Wollstonecraft used her platform at Joseph Johnson's publishing house to take part in the international debate on the slave trade. The anti-slavery cause had ramped up in Britain and France in the wake of the 1789 revolution in Paris.'

The review of Equiano's book was the first of several reviews attributed to Wollstonecraft that dealt with the question of slavery. Another title she reviewed was French journalist Jacques-Pierre Brissot's account of his travels to America. She found much to admire in that book and wrote, 'he writes like an enlightened citizen of the world, whose zeal for liberty appears to arise from the purest moral principles and most expansive humanity', and then added, '[b]ut his humanity is particularly conspicuous in the long account he gives of the treatment of slaves and the attempts made by the Quakers to abolish that infamous traffic' (1789, vol 1, 391).

Wollstonecraft was also aware of the developments in the French colonies, in particular of Saint Domingue (later Haiti). She was an early reader of Brissot and he was the co-founder of the Société des Amis des Noirs, a group of politicians and philosophers, numbering Condorcet and Mirabeau, fighting for the abolition of slavery. During her stay in Paris, she met Brissot, and it is likely that he and his wife, Félicité Brissot, were responsible for the well-received translation of her *Vindication of the Rights of Woman* published in France shortly before Wollstonecraft arrived in Paris in the winter of 1792 (Bour 2022).

Wollstonecraft was definitely involved with the anti-abolitionist movements of her time. But how deep did her concern for enslaved Africans go? In the case of Olympe de Gouges, even though she declared herself entirely won over to the cause of the enslaved Africans from childhood, she was offended when they rebelled against the white planters and started a revolution which proved as violent as the one that had happened (and was still happening in France) (Bergès 2022a). With a degree of disingenuousness, it seems Gouges complained that the Africans should have waited for the new French government to grant them their freedom. Why was it disingenuous? Because already she was questioning the effectiveness of that government, the motives of the men behind it, and the virtue of the people who had fought for the revolution in the streets. She also seems to have had unrealistic expectations of the enslaved Africans, arguing that they must be more virtuous than the French because they were 'closer to nature' and thus further away from the corrupting influence of civil society. So while Gouges did not at any point recant her views that slavery was an evil that needed to be abolished immediately (contrary to many of her contemporaries who thought it should be abolished slowly, in Condorcet's case over a period of seventy years), she nonetheless showed that her commitment to black Africans was tainted by a form of racism which held them up to higher standards than white people and gave her the right to judge them when they fell from these standards.

Did Wollstonecraft fare any better than Gouges? Did she think that, just like the oppressed French people, the enslaved African had a right to rebel? Did she, as Olympe de Gouges did in 1791, baulk at the violence of the Haitian Revolution? We have unfortunately no indication of her views on the Haitian Revolution – if she wrote about it, then those texts were either lost or among the many letters that were destroyed by family and friends so that Godwin would not publish them (Botting 2021, 1311, note 1). It is likely that texts on abolitionism would have proven unpopular and dangerous with her more conservative sisters. When Gouges's son handed Napoleon his mother's writings on abolition, he lost his military post, and – at least according to his own son – it was for abolitionism that ruined her family's prospects.[6] While the British government was still set on slavery – the slave trade was abolished in 1807, but slavery itself only in 1833 – it may have seemed unpolitical to brag about a dead sister's abolitionist views. But this is all speculation and we do not, in fact, have any textual evidence beyond the few references to the enslaved Africans in the two *Vindications*.

There were other ways to be Eurocentric or racist in the eighteenth century than express the wrong views about transatlantic slavery. And here it is easier to catch Wollstonecraft wrong-footed. She speaks – following her mentor and model Catharine Macaulay – of the oppression of 'eastern women' without bothering, it seems, to find out much, if anything, about their actual lives. Wollstonecraft's references to the 'eastern women' living in a 'haram' are, on the whole, citations from Rousseau. Rousseau claims that a European woman should 'cultivate her agreeable talents, in order to please her future husband, with as much care and assiduity as a young Circassian cultivates hers, to fit her for the Haram of an Eastern bashaw' (Wollstonecraft 2014, 112).

---

[6] From a letter printed in Edouard Forestié, *Olympe de Gouges* printed by the author in Montauban 1901, 96–7, my translation.

Wollstonecraft disagrees, but without questioning Rousseau's characterization of the Circassian woman.

When Wollstonecraft refers to women in the Muslim world, she portrays them as the victims of the worst sort of patriarchy which has rendered them 'mere animals' that are 'only fit for a seraglio [harem]' (Wollstonecraft 2014, 32) and as women who 'supinely dream life away in the lap of pleasure' (55). This is not seen as the effect of chance, but blamed on the religion itself: in her introduction she complains that in recent books, 'in the true style of Mahometanism, [women] are treated as a kind of subordinate beings, and not as a part of the human species, when improveable reason is allowed to be the dignified distinction which raises men above the brute creation, and puts a natural scepter in a feeble hand' (30). Later, commenting on Milton, she wonders whether 'in the true Mahometan strain, he meant to deprive us of souls, and insinuate that we were beings only designed by sweet attractive grace, and docile blind obedience, to gratify the senses of man when he can no longer soar on the wing of contemplation' (46).

Wollstonecraft's very negative (and ignorant) take on Islam may have been influenced not only by Rousseau but also by Catharine Macaulay, who wrote in her *Letters on Education*:

> I intend to breed my pupils up to act a rational part in the world, and not to fill up a niche in the seraglio of a sultan, I shall certainly give them leave to use their reason in all matters which concern their duty and happiness, and shall spare no pains in the cultivation of this only sure guide to virtue. (138)

Wollstonecraft saw oriental women as beyond help – much as English aristocratic women were. She also, perhaps, did not feel that saving them from their enervating harems was her responsibility. People were enslaved in the Caribbeans because the British had brought them there, and relied on their free labour controlled by torture to 'sweeten their cups' with sugar and other luxuries. Wollstonecraft had reason, as a British woman who benefitted from the economic advantages of slavery for Britain, to fight for the emancipation of those who were exploited for it. So it is understandable that she would make more of an effort when writing about enslaved African men and women than she did when writing about Ottoman women. But why did she not do more? Why, as someone who cared for justice, did she choose to privilege the cause of white women over that of enslaved Africans? This may be a somewhat unfair criticism given that she died at the age of thirty-eight. For a quick comparison: Simone de Beauvoir did not even begin to think about feminism until she was thirty-eight. Given Wollstonecraft's record, it is likely she would have taken up more causes to fight for had she lived longer.

Wollstonecraft on Gender and Sexual Orientation

One final question about the limits of Wollstonecraft's feminism is how she dealt with issues of gender and sexual orientation. Mostly, she did not. 'Gender' as a concept had not been introduced and clearly separated from that of 'sex'. And questions of LGBTIQ+ rights were not on the table.[7] The fact that Wollstonecraft spoke of 'Sex' rather than 'Gender' might mark her, to some readers, as a gender essentialist, that is, someone who believed that to be born with a sexed body came with a number of innate character traits that could determine a social role. In the case of Wollstonecraft, this seems to be both absolutely wrong and absolutely right, and therefore there is plenty of room for discussion and disagreement.

The reason why it seems absolutely wrong to read Wollstonecraft as a gender essentialist is because she makes the point, on numerous occasions, that men and women are only different in physical terms – and even then it is not clear how committed she really is to men's physical superiority – but that their true nature, their soul, is modelled on the soul of God and therefore not gendered. Much of her disagreement with Rousseau in the *Vindication of the Rights of Woman* touches on the consequence of this view of women's education: if women have a soul, if they can reason, then they must be educated in the same manner as men, and not kept ignorant for the sole purpose of turning them into superficial and pleasing companions for men. Women, Wollstonecraft forcefully argues, have the same potential as men to benefit society through the same kind of contributions, but unless

---

[7] Which is not to say that there was no intellectual LGBTIQ+ community, nor that they were not engaged in trying to philosophize about their place in society: see Maya de Leo 2021.

they too are educated, instead of fulfilling that potential they will harm the progress of human society, for they will – as political animals – meddle from a place of ignorance.

If there are very few real differences between male and female humans, why, one might ask Wollstonecraft, do women look and act so differently from men? Here Wollstonecraft has powerful answers, in which she might be said to anticipate Beauvoir's claim that one is not born but becomes a woman (Bracewell 2019). Wollstonecraft takes pains to show how women's education, or lack thereof, impresses on them the manners we call feminine. Women are not born fainting, or weak of body – they are simply not given the right sort of physical education and they are made to wear clothes that prevent them from breathing properly. Women are not born silly or afraid of mice – they are taught that they should act that way and rewarded early on for girly behaviour.

These acute observations are why Wollstonecraft – when she wants to help women become free – asks for a 'revolution in female manners' rather than a new legislation. Women need rights (and Wollstonecraft promises that she will get on to this in the second volume of the *Vindication* – she never wrote it), but in order to enjoy these rights to the full, they must be able to act like the reasonable and fully functional human beings they are, not like weak and unintelligent dolls.

This is why we should absolutely not read Wollstonecraft as a gender essentialist. But there is another side of the coin, namely: her insistence that motherhood is the 'grand duty' of women, which leads her to claim that a mother who does not properly care for her children (which includes nursing them herself) does not deserve the title of citizen (Wollstonecraft 2014, 181). These comments are problematic, and for some readers they might suffice to persuade them that Wollstonecraft is not ready to separate sex from gender.[8] Others, however, have argued that this is in fact an uncharitable conclusion to draw, for a number of reasons. Firstly, Wollstonecraft does not claim that all women ought to become mothers, but only that those who do should care for their children. Secondly, Wollstonecraft is just as committed to fathers fulfilling their roles as she is to mothers doing so. And in fact, she

---

[8] On this, see my (2013) and Brace (2000).

notes that until fathers take their parental responsibilities seriously, there is no reason to expect mothers to do so. In an unbalanced relationship, it is not possible for the subordinate to take the lead in changing the rhythm and substance of family life. But, of course, men are not expected to nurse babies, and so their role is never going to be equal to women's mothering work.

So here is the third point: Wollstonecraft's insistence that mothers feed their infants themselves is not part of a Rousseauian fangirl programme. She is aware of the risks to infants who are sent out to wet nurses, and in the eighteenth century, there were simply no viable alternatives to breastfeeding. All in all, Wollstonecraft's exalted praise of motherhood as a grand duty doesn't amount to much more than saying parents should do their best to care for their children, and put their children's health before their own desire for entertainment. This is not gendered, and if a little demanding/bossy, not actually objectionable.

It seems as though Wollstonecraft believes that the differences in physical strength would not amount to much if men's and women's bodies were trained in the same way. She does believe that womanhood is a marker of motherhood as babies must be breastfed. But she does not believe that all motherhood is a marker of womanhood in the same sense. She is firm that not all women should have to become mothers, or wives, but that they should be free to pursue independent, professional lives – which at the time would have been incompatible with motherhood. Moreover, she also had stringent requirements for fathers. They should be present, they should avoid dissipation, and they should take their responsibility as educators seriously. A child could only be properly nurtured in a home where they were loved and where healthy emotions and relationships were modelled for them. The book of lessons she wrote for her toddler, Fanny, while she was pregnant with her second child, Mary, shows how this would work in practice: while Papa (who suffered from narcolepsy) rested, the child was encouraged to come to her mother. But when her mother was nursing a migraine, she had to be quiet and go play outside with Papa.[9] While the family picture she draws is in many senses heteronormative,

---

[9] See Lessons in 1989 vol 5.

it is also more egalitarian than most families at the time she was writing, or even now. And as she does not assign gendered roles to Mama or Papa, it is easy to see how her model could slip out of heteronormativity with ease. Indeed, one of the possible endings of her unfinished novel, *Maria or the Wrongs of Woman*, has Maria, her daughter, and Jemima setting up home together, away from men and the world.

So granted that Wollstonecraft probably was not a gender essentialist, how did she fare in terms of LGBTQI+ inclusion? Here we have to read between the lines because there certainly was not a movement of any sort towards the inclusion of people whose sexual orientation or gender identity differed from the cis-gendered and heterosexual. Wollstonecraft does seem at times as if she would disapprove of homosexuality. She suggests that sexual practices that take place in dormitories for single-sex schools ought to be discouraged. But this might simply be a reluctance to allow children to have too many early sexual experiences, and a plea for them to have some privacy. When it comes to adult preferences, it is harder to tell what she may have thought. According to her husband, her relationship with her best friend, Fanny, was a romantic one. He does not say it was a sexual one, and we have no reason to think it would have been, but it was certainly a very intense and exclusive relationship.

It is also worth noting that while Wollstonecraft lived before the question of trans men and women became part of the public debate in England, she seemed to have some views on it. In the *Vindication of the Rights of Woman*, she refers to Madame d'Eon as an exemplary woman, along with Catherine Macaulay and Heloise of Argenteuil. Madame d'Eon was a trans woman, and it was well known at the time, as she had been exiled to England from France and made a living fighting with swords while dressed fully as a woman. While we shouldn't read too much into this, it is noteworthy that Wollstonecraft was happy to add Madame d'Eon to the ranks of womanhood. And it certainly goes together with her disdain of arguments that would assert men's superiority over women for reasons of bodily strength. While the *Vindication of the Rights of Woman* is peppered with sentences assuring men that they are probably physically superior, it also contains arguments for the physical education of girls, and for the view that girls' bodies are only weak because they are not exercised.

Wollstonecraft and the Seeds of Intersectional Feminism?

Was Mary Wollstonecraft an intersectional feminist? Was she a decolonialist before decolonialization? These questions should come with a strong anachronism warning. No one in the eighteenth century was sufficiently aware of the differences in oppressions relating to class, race, gender, or sexual orientation to be in a position even to conceive of intersectionality. Even while there was already a greater variety of voices than we often suppose – there were transwomen writers (Madame D'Eon), black women writers (Phillis Wheatley, Mary Prince), and women writers from lower classes (Olympe de Gouges was born into the family of a butcher) – they were not widely recognized as the representatives of an oppressed group, and there was no effort to understand how the oppressions of each group interacted with other types of oppressions. Mary Prince talks about why being an enslaved woman is different from being an enslaved man – and different from a free woman – even though she perceives that they are all oppressed, but this is a rare occurrence and one that is not part of the language of philosophers thinking about freedom (Prince 1831, 13).

It's unlikely that intersectionality of race, class, and gender (let alone sexual orientation) was properly conceptualized by philosophers until at least the nineteenth century, when Anna Julia Cooper wrote about black women's contribution to understanding oppression and progress. But Wollstonecraft does at least attempt to take into account the different ways in which women in different classes and different parts of the world suffer from oppression. Her *Maria* is an attempt at showing how these differences make it harder for them to communicate and help each other, but how, ultimately, successful communication between an upper-class and a lower-class woman who are both oppressed can lead to a better understanding of oppression and a richer, more satisfying life. So while it is important to understand how eighteenth-century feminists contributed in many ways to the creation of what we now call 'white feminism' and to the oppression of women from the global south, we should also mine feminist texts that were written before these things happened for possible arguments that could have prevented them from happening. The world needn't have gone the way it did, and knowing that philosophers who were excluded from the 'canon' could have helped make it different, or better, is a good reason to study the history of philosophy. Reading Wollstonecraft is one way we can understand this: her work is not simply about the rights of white middle-class English women, but she challenges us to think further, to those who were enslaved in the colonies, those who were different through gender and sexual orientation, and those who belonged to the poorer classes of society. Reading her today teaches us that intersectionality is not just a new concept, but one that any serious defender of rights will have to think their way through, whether or not they have the vocabulary to call it that.

CHAPTER 3

The Caged Life

In Chapter 2, we looked at the boundaries of Wollstonecraft's philosophical concern when it comes to women's subjugation: does it extend to all women, and does it take in all the forms of oppression we think matter? This leads naturally to questions about what Wollstonecraft meant by oppression, and to a discussion of her analysis of the psychology of submission and domination. Here I look at detailed arguments presented in *A Vindication of the Rights of Woman* as well as discussions of examples which again show the range of the women Wollstonecraft considered in her two novels, *Mary, a Fiction* and *Maria or the Wrongs of Woman*. Her philosophical account of domination presages both Simone de Beauvoir's discussion of false consciousness and Amartya Sen's concept of adaptive preferences, but, I will argue, differs significantly from both.

A(N) (In)Dependent Young Woman

Mary, a Fiction was Wollstonecraft's first novel (the only one she completed) and the second book she published, the first being a small treatise on education entitled *Thoughts on the Education of Daughters* (1787). Wollstonecraft wrote *Mary* while she was living in Ireland, taking a break from running her school in Newington Green to earn money as a governess for an aristocratic family. It was printed only once during her lifetime, and, according to a letter she wrote to her sister Everina ten years after its publication, she considered it 'a crude production, and [I] do not very willingly put it in the way of people whose good opinion, as a writer, I wish for; but you may have it to make up the sum of laughter' (Wollstonecraft 1979, 385).

Mary is a semi-autobiographical novel that follows the life of a young woman born to a well-off family (better off than Wollstonecraft's own) with parents very much like the author's own: a mother who is negligent of her daughter and cares only for her son, a father who is a violent alcoholic. Like the author, the heroine is left to fend for herself – to roam the countryside and read whatever she can get her hands on. This provides her, accidentally, with an education that is very close to the one recommended by Rousseau in his *Emile*, where he argues that a child should be left to discover things for himself (his subject here is definitely male) and not have his head stuffed with facts or words he does not understand.

Wollstonecraft had read Rousseau's *Emile* in Ireland, and the influence is clear. In the preface she says that her book is meant to illustrate that 'a genius will educate itself', and the title page contains a quote from Rousseau saying that virtue is all the nourishment a genius requires to grow (1989, vol 1, 35, 37). Another influence from Rousseau was perhaps his *Julie, or the New Heloise*, featuring the passionate and intellectual Julie, who abandons a forbidden love to lead her life as a virtuous and obedient daughter, wife, and mother. Like Julie, Mary has strong and firm emotions and is not easily subdued, except by the possibility that what she is doing is not virtuous. Also like Julie, once she is married, she manages to keep her love interest in another man at the level of deep friendship. But unlike her, she does not easily adapt to marriage, and once she is married, she manages for a while to find a way to live without her husband. While Julie bends dutifully to her father's will, Mary's reaction to forced marriage is violent disgust, an attitude thoroughly consistent with Wollstonecraft's later reference to marriage as legal prostitution (2014, 177). But even Mary, at the end, cannot escape the lot of the woman given to a man in marriage by her father as a business transaction. The heroine accepts her fate and waits patiently for death.

Wollstonecraft's second novel, *Maria or the Wrongs of Woman*, was unfinished when she died, and published posthumously with notes and drafts of suggested endings by her husband Godwin. This novel was, according to its author, motivated by 'the desire of exhibiting the misery and oppression, peculiar to women, that arise out of the partial laws and customs of society' (1989, Vol 1, 83). Its two heroines – aristocratic Maria and, illegitimate child of a lowly servant, Jemima – find their paths crossing and together try to free themselves from the life of oppression they have suffered. Maria married an abusive man who gambled away her money and then attempted to prostitute her to pay his debts. When she ran away with their child, he captured her, took the baby from her, and had Maria locked up in a private asylum. Jemima was born in the lowest ranks of society: the illegitimate child of a lowly servant. She was abandoned, abused, raped, and worked as a prostitute until she found employment as Maria's jailor. Both women fight back against their oppression as best as they can, first separately, and later with each other's help. In one of the suggested endings to the book, Maria and Jemima find Maria's lost daughter and decide to make a life together. Jemima had already escaped from her condition – that of childhood abuse, neglect, poverty, and forced prostitution – through the strength of her determination and intellect (and a bit of luck). But she had not found a place for herself in the world until she allied herself with Maria and fought on her behalf. Maria, on the other hand, truly escapes her abusive husband, and then the hospital where he had her imprisoned. But these two women have lost so much in their fight for freedom and independence that they can hardly be held up as models for other women.

Mary, Maria, and Jemima are all strong intelligent women who value freedom and understand that their humanity means that they are owed freedom in the same way as the men they know. All three are willing to take great risks to escape the fate of dependence in marriage or servitude. All three are capable of forming strong friendships with other women, and have a good moral compass. In a Hollywood movie, they would win. The end of the story would see them living a simple yet rich life in the countryside, surrounded by children and other women, and chuckling lightly when they remember the unpleasant fate met by their would-be oppressors. But in Wollstonecraft's novel, they do not. The endings are dark (and in the case of the alternative endings of *Maria*, different shades of dark). Wollstonecraft does not believe that even with all their virtues her heroines can shake off their chains, 'seize' their freedom, and flourish in their new independent lives.

The lesson from the novels is not pleasant to hear: even the very best women cannot succeed in achieving independence, because laws, institutions, and social prejudice are stacked against them. The best a woman can do is help defeat these obstacles – not take them on singlehandedly, Rambo-style, but become part of a large-scale effort to reform society, so that women may one day achieve independence. And this is, of course, exactly what Wollstonecraft does in her writings, encouraging readers to think differently about the education of children, of young women, about marriage, parenthood, citizenship, and standards of health and beauty.

Women, she says, may value independence, but they don't get to exercise it except in the most restricted circumstances. Jemima, telling her life story to Maria, gives the following example:

> Detesting my nightly occupation, though valuing, if I may so use the word, my independence, which only consisted in choosing the street in which I should wander, or the roof, when I had money, in which I should hide my head, I was some time before I could prevail on myself to accept of a place in a house of ill fame, to which a girl, with whom I had accidentally conversed in the street, had recommended me. (1989, Vol 1, 112)

Jemima is aware that her story is only marginally about independence: whether she is working on the streets or in a brothel, she is still a prostitute, at the mercy of men and unprotected. Once she is settled in her job as a jailor for the asylum, she sees another path to independence: the money she is able to save (1989, Vol 1, 89). But even this comes at a cost: that of ignoring the plight of those, like Maria, who are wrongly interned. The men in *Mary* and *Maria* have a very different perspective on what it means to be independent. Henry Darnford in *Maria* tells how he travelled the world in pursuit of independence, and Mary's husband chooses to do the same as soon as he becomes his own master, leaving his new wife – to her great relief – to fend for herself. This is a stark contrast with Maria's imprisonment or Jemima's life on the streets. Even Mary's freedom is dependent on her husband's good will. When he tires of travelling, he calls her back to his side and she has no choice but to obey.

But did Wollstonecraft herself not achieve the independence that Mary, Maria, and Jemima craved? She seems to claim that she has, in the opening paragraph of the *Vindication of the Rights of Woman*:

> Independence I have long considered as the grand blessing of life, the basis of every virtue – and independence I will ever secure by contracting my wants, though I were to live on a barren heath. (2014, 21)

Yet she is aware that her actual independence is fragile and bound to certain contingencies – such as the fact that she was not forced to marry, or under the control of a male relative. The only one of her brothers who could have claimed control over her was quite happy, it seems, to have nothing to do with her.[1] She was also lucky to have found a reliable and fair employer in Joseph Johnson, who gave her the opportunity to become 'the first of a new genus', that is, the first person to earn regular wages as a writer. And although she did twice become pregnant outside of marriage – going against social prejudice – the first time she pretended to be married (Imlay, the father of her child, had her registered as his wife with the US embassy, so that she would not be arrested as an English citizen in Paris) and the second she decided to marry for good, so as not to encounter too much social ire. This is not to say that the level of independence Wollstonecraft achieved as a woman in the eighteenth century was not truly impressive, but to indicate that she herself was aware of the fragility of her achievements and did not hold other women to the standards she felt she had reached partly through luck.

The Bird in the Cage and the Bars Only It Can See

Wollstonecraft's story about independence is complicated. On the one hand, she tells us in the *Vindication of the Rights of Woman* that she cannot live without it, but on the other, in her novels she paints the lives of women who value independence as much as she does and yet utterly fail to obtain it.

---

[1] Edward Wollstonecraft, who'd inherited part of the family business from his grandfather, had arranged a marriage between his close friend and sister Eliza. However, Eliza claimed that her husband was abusing her and appealed to her sister, who helped her escape. She helped her other brothers make a living, in the army and abroad (Charles travelled to America and his wife, Nancy Wollstonecraft, became a writer on women's rights). A fourth brother, Henry, is unaccounted for and possibly was incarcerated in an asylum as a young man.

Clearly, valuing independence is not sufficient to obtain it. And as the story of Jemima illustrates, there is something horrifyingly pathetic about attempts to maintain independence when one has nothing: for Jemima it meant resisting making the switch from working as a street prostitute to joining a brothel: either way, she would be horribly abused (1989, Vol 1, 112).

What we need, then, to fill the gap between this absolute confidence that independence is valuable and women's utter lack of it is an explanation of what it is that stops women from acquiring independence. One passage that stands out in the *Vindication of the Rights of Woman* when we are seeking an explanation of why women do not simply seize their independence is this one:

> Confined then in cages like the feathered race, they have nothing to do but to plume themselves, and stalk with mock majesty from perch to perch. It is true they are provided with food and raiment, for which they neither toil nor spin; but health, liberty, and virtue, are given in exchange. But, where, amongst mankind, has been found sufficient strength of mind to enable a being to resign these adventitious prerogatives; one who, rising with the calm dignity of reason above opinion, dared to be proud of the privileges inherent in man? And it is vain to expect it whilst hereditary power chokes the affections and nips reason in the bud. (2014, 83)

Rich women, she says, are kept in metaphorical cages, like luxury pets, asked only to entertain through their song and beauty, but inconsequential and easily ignored – one can leave the room, or cover the cage with a cloth. Their rewards also reflect their lack of importance. They are fed, which will keep them alive, and they are given the kind of things that will enhance their attractiveness and power to entertain: pretty clothes and jewellery. That these are valued by women seems to show that they enjoy their role as mere entertainers, and that they perceive the gifts they are given as truly worth having, more so than freedom, health, and virtue would be. This is what led philosopher and economist Amartya Sen to think of Wollstonecraft as a predecessor of his theory of Adaptive Preferences, that is, the view that in very harsh circumstances people may come to adapt their preferences so that they value the small things they are given more than the big necessary things they know they cannot have. Adaptive preferences can also be understood as a form of existentialist bad faith of the sort that Sartre and Beauvoir attributed to those who failed, for one reason or another, to live authentic lives. But before we go into this, let's take a closer look at Wollstonecraft's cage analogy and its implications for women's freedom.

Wollstonecraft offers the following explanation of why most women do not simply break free from oppression and seek their independence: very few people, she says, have sufficient strength of mind to resist the life of luxury that is being offered to those caged women, and if they did, then that strength would be sapped anyway by 'hereditary power'. What does she mean? Strength of mind is not something that one is born with – although some may be born with a greater propensity to develop it than others. A genius, she wrote about her novel *Mary*, will educate itself (1898, vol I, 35), and therefore will eventually acquire strength of mind and the desire for independence. But the title page of the novel itself conveys a slightly different message, a quotation from Rousseau to the effect that it is through the exercise of virtue that a genius will develop: '*L'exercice des plus sublimes vertus élève et nourrit le génie*' ('It is by exercising the highest virtues that genius is raised and nourished' 1989, vol I, 1). But can a caged genius that is only taught to look and sound pretty exercise the most sublime virtues? It is unlikely, as the exercise of virtues does require some sort of interaction with others that goes beyond mere performance. It requires a deeper connection than that afforded by flirting, and it requires the exercise of one's faculties, especially reason, but these, Wollstonecraft tells us, are 'nipped in the bud' by 'hereditary power'.

The expression 'nipped in the bud' brings to mind another metaphor Wollstonecraft likes to use when describing women's mis-education, that of the hot-house:

> Men and women should not have their sensations heightened in the hot-bed of luxurious indolence, at the expense of their understanding; for unless there be a ballast of understanding, they will never become either virtuous or free: an aristocracy, founded on property or sterling talents, will ever sweep before it, the alternately timid, and ferocious, slaves of feeling. (2014, 96)[2]

For women in the hot-house, in particular, the only aspects of their faculties that are developed are those that are useful to their oppressors,

---

[2] A hot-bed was the eighteenth-century equivalent of the hot-house, a pit filled with horse manure and covered with glass.

so that the development is only partial, and therefore the whole remains fragile, much like a hot-house flower that has been stripped of its leaves so that the head may grow. Such a being is not meant to survive, or to thrive in the world, but is merely an ornament or the means to continue a lineage:

> And when, to render the present state more complete, though every thing proves it to be but a fraction of a mighty sum, she is incited by present gratification to forget her grand destination, nature is counteracted, or she was born only to procreate and rot. (90)

'Hereditary power' is, of course, what we now call the patriarchy – the power that men have over women just because they are born men – and at the same time it is social hierarchy, the powers that the rich and the titled have over the common people and the poor. But it is also the institutionalized aspect of patriarchy and class – the fact that laws and institutions favour rich men and regard women as their property, and, finally, the social prejudices that ensure that the patriarchal values stay in place.

Let us look again at one of Wollstonecraft's fictionalized case studies, *Mary, a Fiction*, to see how she sees these forces operate.

Mary, the heroine of Wollstonecraft's first novel, does not grow up in a cage. Her neglect by her parents means that she learns a lot more than she would have had she been educated:

> [S]he would ramble about the garden, admire the flowers, and play with the dogs. An old house-keeper told her stories, read to her, and, at last, taught her to read. Her mother talked of enquiring for a governess when her health would permit; and, in the interim desired her own maid to teach her French. As she had learned to read, she perused with avidity every book that came in her way. Neglected in every respect, and left to the operations of her own mind, she considered every thing that came under her inspection, and learned to think. (1989, Vol 1, 10)

She is not taught to dress and behave like a lady, because her mother is mostly uninterested in her education, and because the model she provides is thoroughly unattractive. Had the mother been a fascinating creature, things might have gone differently. But the mother in the novel comes across as a weak, silly, and boring creature, not one that a bright little girl would ever want to emulate. Mary's reason, therefore, while it is not cared for and nourished by the adults in her life, is not nipped in the bud but left to grow in its own wild ways, checked only by experience.

But while Mary's reason was not 'nipped in the bud', this was not enough to ensure an unfettered growth. Mary was constrained in her development by the hereditary powers of patriarchy. In the first instance, her father married her off to a friend's son in order to settle a dispute over part of her inheritance. Neither Mary nor her husband-to-be had any say in the matter, which was agreed over drinks between the two fathers (Wollstonecraft 1989, vol, 18). But once married, Mary no longer had any say in anything, while her husband had a say over every part of her life as well as his own. She has to ask permission from her husband in order to travel to Portugal, where she hopes her friend will recover from consumption. He agrees, because he too wants to travel and will be able to do so more easily if he does not have a wife waiting for him at home. Later, when her friend is dead and she is back in England, she tells the family she is staying with 'that she had a reason for not living with her husband, which must some time remain a secret' (55) and she vows to herself, 'I will work, she cried, do any thing rather than be a slave' (55). A short while later she receives a letter from her husband telling her he does not wish to go home yet as he wants to travel still (63). When eventually she meets him (they had met briefly for the marriage ceremony only), she finds out that he is a 'good-natured but weak man', which does nothing to stop her fundamental disgust of her married condition. Even after a year of life together, his taking her hand causes her to 'feel a sickness, a faintness at her heart, and wish, involuntarily, that the earth would open and swallow her' (72) so that eventually she grows to hope that her health will fail her and that this will hasten her to 'that world *where there is neither marrying,* nor giving in marriage' (73).

Mary's husband is amiable and not particularly bright, and he is young enough when they marry to care more about his own freedom of movement than controlling his wife's. But that changes, and once he decides that he should settle, so must she, no matter how much she wants to be away from him. Even her friends collude in her fate. The family she stayed with and had fobbed off with a 'secret reason' why she could not live with her husband were shocked that she stayed so long away from him, even though they were the beneficiaries of her charity.

The well-meaning 'friend' who takes an interest in Mary's fate and story is also the instrument of her 'reconciliation' with her husband. He hears her objections to married life, and responds by telling her he knows her husband to be a decent person, and bringing him to see Mary. She faints as her husband approaches her (1989, vol 1, 71).

Mary, despite being in full control of her reason, cannot therefore escape the cage. Or rather, she may be under the impression, as a child, that she has escaped it, as she takes long walks or visits her friend Ann, and later when she persuades her husband to let her travel. But she is brutally recalled to the awareness of her cage, first by her father marrying her off and then by her friends and acquaintances forcing her to go back to her husband. And finally, her husband, when he revokes the temporary authorization he'd granted her to live apart from him, locks the door of the cage and throws away the key. Mary, it appears, had never left the cage. She thought she was roaming the world freely, but the bars of the cage were always there, keeping her from her freedom.

How can a person fail to see that they are in a cage? How can Mary, an intelligent young woman, have ever believed she had a shot at independence? Philosopher Marilyn Frye explains this phenomenon when she likens oppression to a 'network of forces and barriers that exposes one to loss, penalty or contempt' whenever a woman departs from the path traced for her by patriarchy (Frye 2000, 13). The obstacles do not act individually or discretely, but as part of a multilayered network, so that if we skip one, there are always another two waiting. Frye uses the analogy of the birdcage to make that point:

> Consider a birdcage. If you look very closely at just one wire in the cage, you cannot see the other wires. If your conception of what is before you is determined by this myopic focus, you could look at that one wire, up and down the length of it, and be unable to see why a bird would not just fly around the wire anytime it wanted to go somewhere. Furthermore, even if, one day at a time, you myopically inspected each wire, you still could not see why a bird would have trouble going past the wires to get anywhere. There is no physical property of any one wire, nothing that the closest scrutiny could discover, that will reveal how a bird could be inhibited or harmed by it except in the most accidental way. It is only when you step back, stop looking at the wires one by one, microscopically, and take a macroscopic view of the whole cage, that you can see why the bird does not go anywhere; and then you will see it in a moment. It

will require no great subtlety of mental powers. It is perfectly obvious that the bird is surrounded by a network of systematically related barriers, no one of which would be the least hindrance to its flight, but which, by their relations to each other, are as confining as the solid walls of a dungeon. (2000, 12)

The bars are obvious to us at the end of *Mary, a Fiction*. They are the laws regarding marriage – the fact that a woman cannot own money of her own, that it is hard for her to find work that will sustain her if she does not live with her husband, that her friends and society in general will find it odd, scandalous even, that she lives without her husband, and that they will do everything in their power to bring them back together. At the beginning of the story the bars are not so clearly visible. We think that Mary may make a break for it, that her genius, her intense romantic friendships will help her become the independent woman she dreams of being. But early marriage makes that impossible. It is the first bar of the cage to become apparent, and the others follow. Had it not been for that marriage, would Mary have been free? She might have been to the same extent as her creator, Mary Wollstonecraft, was. But she would still have had to contend with the legal and social infrastructure that prevented women from achieving full independence: lack of citizenship and representation, lack of opportunities, and being at all times the target for gossip and reputation-destroying scandal of the sort that might prevent a woman from making a living – and in fact did stop the sales of Wollstonecraft's books after her death, making it harder for her widower to support her two daughters.[3]

What the novel *Mary* does, then, is show that although a bright and capable nature will assert itself even without access to formal education, this will not suffice to help its owner live an independent life, if that person is a woman. The message from Rousseau that genius will educate itself is optimistic, but at the end of the story, the only hope left to the heroine is that she will die soon and escape her married condition. The bars of the cage are real – Wollstonecraft tells us. They are not the product of our own making or ignorance. They are spread throughout the landscape of our lives, designed to stop any possible attempt at

---

[3] Granted, it was Godwin who revealed the details of his wife's life that led to scandal. But it was Fanny and Mary, Wollstonecraft's daughters, who suffered from the financial fallout.

escape. Virtue cannot break them – but it can allow us, perhaps, to hope for a better afterlife, and one that comes soon. It is not a happy picture.

Adapting to the Caged Life?

Wollstonecraft seems sceptical about individual women's ability to become free in a world riddled with laws, institutions, social practices, and moral prejudices intent on keeping them dependent on men. And she shows us in her two novels that women who do try to break free end up being repressed in ways that they hadn't necessarily anticipated. So Mary is married off to a man she does not know. Maria, of the *Wrongs of Woman*, chose her own husband, but when she realized what a bad choice she had made and attempted to escape with her infant daughter, she was caught, forcibly separated from her daughter, and locked in an asylum for the mentally ill. Her friend and jailor Jemima goes through her life being bounced between social forms of Charybdis and Scylla – abandoned, raped, thrown out in the streets, forced into prostitution – until through sheer luck one of her clients teaches her to read and write and leaves her a small legacy which allows her to go on the job market and eventually become Maria's jailor.

Both Maria and Jemima live through horrendous events, and they do their best to fight their way through them so that they may live a life of their own choosing. They are not in any way deceiving themselves that the things that happen to them are acceptable or normal, nor are they trying to find pleasure in small things to make up for the losses they won't acknowledge. In fact, the main mechanism that would lead to self-deception according to Wollstonecraft, the nipping of reason in the bud, is entirely absent from their stories. Maria tells us that she finds relief in exercising her intellect, while Jemima says: 'the treatment that rendered me miserable, seemed to sharpen my wits' (1989, Vol I, 108). In other words, they are not engaging in what Amartya Sen called 'adaptive preferences', a phenomenon he defines in the following way:

> A thoroughly deprived person, leading a very reduced life, might not appear to be badly off in terms of the mental metric of desire and its fulfillment, if the hardship is accepted with non-grumbling resignation. In situations of longstanding deprivation, the victims do not go on grieving and lamenting all the time, and very often make great effort to

take pleasure in small mercies and to cut down personal desires to modest – 'realistic' – proportions. (Sen 1992, 55)

That Wollstonecraft's unhappy heroines don't display symptoms of adaptive preferences matters for two reasons. Firstly, Sen claims that he was in some ways inspired by Wollstonecraft in coming up with the concept, and secondly, the sort of feminism that relies on the unmodified concept of adaptive preferences tends to be colonial or 'white' feminism, and to give unhelpful accounts of the oppression of women in the global south. So it matters what Wollstonecraft has to say in relation to what Sen called adaptive preferences.

Sen has several times referenced Wollstonecraft in his writing on global justice and the capability approach. In a 2006 piece, he claimed that she had influenced his theory of adaptive preferences:

> I was intellectually influenced, in pursuing this subject, primarily by my other heroes, in particular by Mary Wollstonecraft's analysis of women's evident contentment even in highly unequal circumstances. (Sen 2006, 82)

Elsewhere he writes:

> One particular insight that Mary Wollstonecraft had is the basic commonality of different kinds of social deprivation and societal inequality, which have a uniting *feature*. [. . .]The relevance of feminist thinking is not confined to gender inequality only, nor only to the pursuit of perspectives that a woman's position or a feminist commitment can bring out. It also links with other types of deep inequality. (Sen 2005, 6)[4]

Wollstonecraft does have something that resembles a theory of adaptive preferences (though I prefer to call it 'stunted' preferences).[5] But what is significant is that she sees this not in the women who suffer most or who, in Sen's words, are 'thoroughly deprived' or live 'very reduced lives', but in the lives of women who are rich and relatively well treated by their husbands. The women in the gilded cages are not starving working-class women. They are the valued wives of rich men who are

---

[4] And again in *The Idea of Justice*, Sen refers to Wollstonecraft many times, emphasizing the importance of universal inclusion (Sen 2011, 117) and explaining the force of her style, which consists of indignation backing up reasoned arguments (Sen 2011, 391).
[5] See my 2011.

happy to throw expensive furniture, food, and clothing at them in exchange for their attractive presence in their lives. Of course, they are not valued as human beings. And the goods they receive are not worth what they give in exchange, 'health, liberty and virtue'.[6] But women such as Maria or Jemima are not likely to be tricked into bird-like acceptance by having nice jewels given them. Maria is victim of a violent and depraved husband, while Jemima is used by all who come across her, and struggles to find food and shelter. The very idea that they could be tricked into not recognizing the abuse they suffer is insulting. And this is one of the points made by decolonial feminists against applying the theory of adaptive preferences to the oppression of women in the global south.

Serene Khader has argued that cultural essentialism, and the practice of deriving 'universal' ideals from Western practices then attempting to apply them to non-ideal situations in the global south, results in a failure to appraise women's actual agency (or in Wollstonecraftian terms, independence). Because agency is not seen to operate in the same ways it would be expected to in Western countries, it is thought to have been erased by patriarchal oppression (2017). If we take the example Sen first used to illustrate gendered adaptive preferences, we can see how that works. Women in some poor rural settings in Bangladesh, he observed, eat less than men, and, despite their very obvious malnutrition, claim that they are satisfied with the amount of food they are getting. For Sen, this is evidence that they have internalized their oppression, that they could not bear to contemplate a highly distressing state of affairs that they could do nothing about, and therefore decided to accept it as the norm. While it is useful to see preferences as moving according to situations, rather than set at birth according to a set of norms that are unrelated to culture, personality, or life events, the theory of adaptive preferences as first developed by Sen lacks the sort of subtlety that is needed in giving an accurate account, in particular, of women's oppressions.

People do not always repress preferences when they are not met. Other things must come into consideration. In the case of the

---

[6] Serene Khader also points out that Wollstonecraft's caged birds are not severely deprived (Khader 2015, 355–6), if all that is taken from them is the capacity to be virtuous.

Bangladeshi women who eat less than their husbands, they might simply have reflected that it is better for them and their children if they keep their husbands well fed and happy, because that will make their own lives safer and more comfortable (Khader 2012, 310). These women live in a world regulated by complementarism, a framework which assigns different roles to men and women. While this framework contains many gender injustices, it also comes with its own set of processes for navigating them. Women can make choices that will best enable them to live as well and ensure their children's flourishing, but these choices can only be understood by someone who knows the system. Effecting reforms without trying to understand the system may result in removing from women whatever space they have for making these choices. So what is needed instead is to understand how the complementarist framework of their lives works, and to pay particular attention to the history of this framework and to the role Western colonialists played in making it worse.[7] Working within that system, says Kahder, to bring about changes that will lead the household decision-makers (men) to make better decisions regarding women would not only be more effective but would also show more respect for the existing agency of women who suffer from these injustices.

How does Khader's analysis of gender injustice in the Global South in the twenty-first century help us understand what the women Wollstonecraft describes are going through? The aristocratic women who live their lives as though they are exotic birds in pretty cages also have a particular social framework to contend with, which may make some of their decisions seem more rational. This means that there are similar reasons to think that the adaptive preferences theory fails to describe their situation accurately. Eighteenth-century aristocratic women had to negotiate their position within a particular social framework, one in which they could only have influence – and indeed survive – through men. For some, it made sense for them to choose to play the role of the bird in a cage just for the sake of participating in human life as fully as possible. For others, it may simply have made

---

[7] Part of the decolonial argument is that although gender injustice was never completely absent from the Global South, it was worsened by European colonists who imposed their own views of gender and complementarity on the countries they occupied. See Bradford, 1996.

sense to continue to be well fed and live in luxury, as the alternative was to be sent to live in isolation and relative poverty. This is what happened to Maria Rushworth, the eldest daughter of Sir and Lady Bertram in Jane Austen's *Mansfield Park*, when she eloped with her neighbour, Henry Crawford. Her character is deemed 'destroyed' – she can no longer be exhibited in her cage, so she is sent away with her aunt in a country 'remote and private' (Austen 1997, 315). Had she been a good little bird, chirping away for her very dull but rich husband, she would have kept her perch.

The biggest reason why the theory of adaptive preferences is not a very promising way to interpret what Wollstonecraft has to say about women's oppression is the difference between Sen's subjects – poor women in rural Bangladesh – and Wollstonecraft's own. In Wollstonecraft's accounts, women who do seem to adapt their preferences are generally not living in thoroughly deprived conditions, while those who genuinely suffer seem to be quite well aware that they do. Perhaps what Wollstonecraft has to say about women who pretend to themselves that all is fine when they are in fact deprived of their capacity to exercise freedom, reason, or virtue is better looked at in terms of the existentialist concept of bad faith, and in particular its feminist incarnation in Simone de Beauvoir's *The Second Sex*.

Bad Faith and Relative Freedom

Bad faith as an existentialist concern was first discussed in print by Sartre in *Being and Nothingness*. The concept he develops there owes more to that of sour grapes, that is, the propensity one has to deceive oneself rather than face an unpleasant reality, than it does to adaptive preferences, which tend to happen when one suffers from severe deprivation. What this means is that Sartre tends to equate bad faith with moral weakness rather than oppression. This is most problematic when it comes to cases where oppression is also in play. One of Sartre's examples in particular stands out. It concerns a woman who is, to all intents and purposes, being sexually harassed.

> Let us take, for example, this woman who has arrived at a first meeting. She knows full well the intentions entertained, in relation to her, by the

man speaking to her. She also knows that sooner or later she will have to make a decision. But she does not want to feel its urgency: she takes account only of the respectful and discreet aspects of her partner's attitude. She does not see his behavior as an attempt to make the so-called opening moves; in other words, she does not want to see the possibilities of development over time that his behavior presents; she confines his activity to what it is in the present, and has no wish to read, in the sentences he addresses to her, anything but their explicit meaning. If he says 'I admire you so much,' she strips this sentence of its sexual background: she attaches immediate meanings – envisaged as objective properties – to her interlocutor's sayings and actions. [...]But now he takes her hand. This action by her interlocutor threatens to change the situation by calling for an immediate decision: to leave her hand there is to consent, herself, to the flirtation; it commits her. To withdraw it is to disrupt the vague and unstable harmony that gave the moment its charm. The moment of decision needs to be deferred for as long as possible. We know what happens now: the young woman leaves her hand where it is but she does not notice she has left it there. She does not notice because it turns out by chance that she is, at that moment, pure spirit. She takes her interlocutor right up to the most elevated regions of sentimental speculation, she talks about life, her life, and she shows herself in her most essential aspect: as a person, a consciousness. And while she does this, the divorce of body from soul is accomplished: her hand rests there, inert between the hot hands of her partner, neither consenting nor resisting – a thing.

We will say that this woman is in bad faith. (Sartre 2018, 97–8)

Sartre's discussion rankles. He is basically calling the woman a tease. To say that she 'knows' she has to make a choice is tantamount to saying that it is the man's right to set the agenda and that the woman has no choice but to conform to it. And if she doesn't, then she is seen as dishonest, or playing a game. Sartre is probably right that the woman in question, the one who stepped into that bar to meet her date when he and Beauvoir were there, does have to make a choice. The patriarchal situation she is in requires her to fit in with the man's agenda. This is what is expected of her, and this is what she has been taught she ought to do. At the same time, she knows that her choice will limit her life further: if she turns him down, she will not be able to enjoy the rest of the evening, and may acquire a reputation such that other men do not ask her out, which will mean that, as a French woman in the 1940s, she may not be able to go out at all. If, on the other hand, she says yes, then she will end up either married to him or having an affair, which will make it much harder for her to marry in the future. None of the options are particularly attractive and it makes sense to try to step away from having to make a choice at all.

Like Wollstonecraft's well-off women, the woman in the bar is not thoroughly deprived, but she is nonetheless confined by the bars of a cage that the male observer, in this case Sartre, fails to see, perhaps because he is microscopically focusing on one particular bar – that of bad faith or self-deception. No doubt, self-deception plays a role in the story – it is unlikely that any woman would put herself through this masquerade of a date if she had in the front of her mind all the implications of any move she might or might not make – but it is far from being the biggest obstacle to her freedom.

The concept of bad faith, while so often associated with *Being and Nothingness*, was in fact shaped as the result of conversations between Beauvoir and Sartre. Kate Kirkpatrick even suggests that it was Beauvoir's observations that prompted the debate, and that it was she who first developed it in writing in an early draft of her novel *Anne ou Quand Prime le Spirituel* (192). Both Kirkpatrick and Toril Moi also argue that Beauvoir went on, both in her novel *She Came to Stay* and in the *Second Sex*, to develop a different version of bad faith from the one Sartre sets out in *Being and Nothingness* (Moi 2008, 152; Kirkpatrick 2019 192, 209). In her 1943 novel – published the same year as *Being and Nothingness*, Moi notices – Beauvoir relates the very same incident of the couple in the café, but sees it quite differently:

> In another corner [of the bar], a young woman with green and blue feathers in her hair was looking uncertainly at a man's huge hand that had just pounced on hers. (Beauvoir 2006, 80)

The perspective, in Beauvoir's narrative, is that of the woman who is alienated, not from herself and her own desires but by the fact that a man is physically holding her hand captive.

Simone de Beauvoir takes up the concept of bad faith in *The Second Sex*, where she argued that a woman who chooses to find contentment in a domestic life, as a housewife and perhaps also a mother, exhibited bad faith. Women don't really enjoy doing the housework or changing diapers, she said, or if they do, it is because they have forced themselves to stop looking for enjoyment in more rewarding places.

> For maternal devotion can be experienced in perfect authenticity; but in fact, this is rarely the case. Ordinarily, maternity is a strange compromise of narcissism, altruism, dream, sincerity, bad faith, devotion, and cynicism. (Beauvoir 2009,632)

Bad faith for Beauvoir meant something different from what it meant for Sartre. Sartre saw bad faith as using one's situation as an excuse for one's life – 'I am a wife, I can only obey my husband' or 'I am a mother, my nature dictates that I should care for my children.' Sartre, rejecting essentialism, believed that one could always choose to react differently to one's situation, except for one odd bit of essentialism of his own: human beings, he thought, were bound to fall into the category of dominator or dominated. Beauvoir's concept of bad faith was perhaps more radical. As Kirkpatrick tells us, she rejected this form of essentialism too:

> If Sartre thought human beings were by nature doomed to desire domination, then there really was no exit from living our own oppressors. Beauvoir's philosophy, by contrast, refused 'the consolations of lies and resignations' – it was an excuse to think that it's just human nature to dominate or submit. (Kirkpatrick 2019, 214)

This was an ethical disagreement: for Sartre, a woman's bad faith is measured according to her failure to participate in males' projects of seduction (Moi, 2008, 150–4). Beauvoir's ethical stance was, like Sartre's, underlaid by a metaphysical one. Sartre believed that we became free through a situation that we could realize our freedom by transcending that situation. But Beauvoir objected that women's situations were not and could not always be transcended, because they were part of the world that made them who they were, and in many cases, that world made it impossible for them to assert their freedom. Turning away from Sartre's analysis, she went back to Heidegger and the idea that human beings are at one with their world (*Mitsein*) and to Husserl's phenomenology in order to make it clear that it is the lived experience of women, rather than their situation, that we need to focus on in order to help them achieve freedom (see Kirkpatrick 2019, 264).

> But what singularly defines the situation of woman is that being, like all humans, an autonomous freedom, she discovers and chooses herself in a world where men force her to assume herself as Other: an attempt is made to freeze her as an object and doom her to immanence, since her transcendence will be forever transcended by another essential and sovereign consciousness. Woman's drama lies in this conflict between the fundamental claim of every subject, which always posits itself as essential, and the demands of a situation that constitutes her as inessential. How, in the feminine condition, can a human being accomplish herself? What paths are open to her? Which ones lead to dead ends? How can she find independence within dependence? What circumstances limit women's freedom and can she overcome them? (Beauvoir 2009, 37)

Let's come back to the woman in the bar. She does not take her hand away when the man she is with puts his own oversized hand on it, but she does not engage in the flirty behaviour that the man seems to expect. Is she really in a position to 'transcend her facticity'? The fact that she is bound by very strict social rules to behave in certain ways with men while she is still unmarried, the fact that the man here is stronger than her, the fact that she probably rarely gets the chance to have proper conversations with people who are not her parents – all make it very unlikely that she will decide to break free and either tell the man that she'll not sleep with him or that she won't marry him, but would quite like to be friends, or even engage in some non-consequential flirtation. This is what Beauvoir understood when she asked Sartre 'What sort of transcendence could a woman in a harem achieve?' (Beauvoir 1965, 434). Not everyone can seize their freedom by choosing to transcend the situation they are in – it very much depends on the situation. She could have added: it depends on how many bars the situation consists of, and how they are arranged. Sartre, who as we saw focuses microscopically on one bar at a time, fails to see this.

The unwillingness to break free such as that experienced by Wollstonecraft's well-off women, who 'choose' to stay in their cage where they are at least fed and offered a pleasant existence, is not obviously the result of either bad faith or adaptive preferences. It can also be seen as a legitimate choice on their part, one which makes more sense than going against everything to strike out on one's own. This is a point argued by Charlotte Knowles when she questions Daniel

Dennett's statement that 'freedom is an offer we can't refuse' (Knowles 2021, 12). It is just obvious that some women, Knowles says, choose to conform to the submissive role in the way they dress and relate to their bodies. They might be complicit in their own subordination, but it's far from clear how they are complicit (Knowles 2021, 7). The choices that are open to these women may not be as attractive or varied as those of the men they submit to, but they are nonetheless choices they can and do make. And although we see these choices as belonging in a framework of inequality and one in which women submit to men, they vary greatly in degree. Feminists who choose to shave their legs or wear make-up may feel conflicted about why they do it, but they are hardly oppressed and in fact can be empowered in some ways (Hay 2020, 20).

While the things we do to conform to standards of beauty certainly do belong to a system of oppression, within that system, they can sometimes play the role of liberatory acts. In an interview, Dolly Parton explained how her love of outrageously flashy and sexy clothing came about. As a child she had seen a woman wearing what she thought were lovely clothes. 'Who is that?' she asked. 'The town tramp. She is trash.' 'That's what I want to be when I grow up', young Dolly replied, 'trash.'[8] The adult Dolly Parton, far from being a submissive, unfree individual, is a trailblazing artist who has done a lot of work freeing others from the oppression of poverty, through her singing, her acting, and her charity work. Such individuals, perhaps, while they do not break free from the system that oppresses them and their like, work within the system to help generate more freedom in the world.

Whether it is her caged-bird analogy, her anticipation of the concept of adaptive preferences, or of the existentialist account of bad faith, Wollstonecraft's discussion of sexist oppression is clearly not out of touch with what philosophers speak about today. But what else does it bring us? Because she puts all these things together, she is able to offer a very vivid account of what it means to be a woman and to be oppressed, even when one appears to be well off and to have agency. She makes it clear why a woman might 'choose' not to fight, why she might 'prefer' to go with the flow of patriarchy, and why that would at

---

[8] Interview for Wire, 5 October 2020, https://youtu.be/Bc9gTqiljLA.

the same time be a less than ideal choice or preference, but still one that we can make sense of, without saying that this woman is somehow irrational. Patriarchy, she says, makes us do things that we'd prefer not to do. It's both our responsibility to try and change the way things are so that we don't do these things, and perfectly understandable that we find it hard, and that very few of us succeed in raising ourselves to fight.

CHAPTER 4

The Body

Wollstonecraft argues that women are shaped to be less than they ought to be. Ultimately, that means less virtuous, and as it is through the exercise of reason that we can become virtuous, the (mis-)shaping of women's reason is a big part of what Wollstonecraft has to talk about. But it is not just reason that helps us become virtuous: a strong, healthy body, she argues, is also conducive to a virtuous life. And her observations lead her to conclude that women's bodies are just as misshapen as their minds. Here we look at how she conceived of the body in education, how she placed importance on the shaping of a strong, healthy body, and how she saw the parental (mostly maternal) body as instrumental in the flourishing of children. This focus on educating bodies as well as minds highlights another way in which Wollstonecraft's thoughts on education, especially those expressed in her *Vindication of the Rights of Woman*, were revolutionary.

Pretty Frocks All Muddied Up: Strength and Health as Learned Traits

In Chapter 3, we saw that the sort of mis-education middle- and upper-class women were typically exposed to in the eighteenth century had the result of weakening their reasoning abilities, and preventing them from seeing their oppression, by bringing them up in a hotbed of luxurious indolence (Wollstonecraft 2014, 96). The same sort of analogy was taken up by Frances Power Cobbe in her review of Mill's *Subjection of Women*. She talks of the unnatural aspect of 'the characters and abilities of creatures manipulated as women are' (Cobbe 1995, 60) and describes the process of the manipulation as follows: 'She may freely grow, and even swell to abnormal proportions in the region of the heart; but the head has but a small chance of expansion and the whole base is weak and rickety to the extreme' (Cobbe 1995, 61). Cobbe is clearly talking both about mind and body, and indeed, to make her point she appeals to an alleged medieval Chinese practice of forcing babies to grow in porcelain jars so that they should take on whatever deformity took the fancy of a Mandarin. Wollstonecraft also uses Chinese customs as a metaphor:

> To preserve personal beauty, woman's glory! the limbs and faculties are cramped with worse than Chinese bands, and the sedentary life which they are condemned to live, whilst boys frolic in the open air, weakens the muscles and relaxes the nerves. (Wollstonecraft 2014, 68)

Putting aside the racism embodied in this seeking of examples in China (rather than medieval Europe, which surely had plenty of atrocities to choose from that would neatly illustrate the same thing), the point seems to be that it is not only the mind but also the bodies of women that are tampered with in their upbringing. This becomes clearest in chapter 3 of the *Vindication*, which is almost entirely concerned with bodily strength and health, and the ways in which women are systematically oppressed by a system of mis-education which keeps their bodies from growing as healthily as they should.

By the time we come to Chapter 3, however, we've already had several notices from Wollstonecraft that she's not going to argue with the claim that women are inferior to men 'with respect to bodily strength' (2014, 32). And here again, she reiterates the point that 'bodily strength seems to give men a natural superiority over women' (65) and that 'strength of body, with some shew of reason, is the boast of men' (66). Given such statements of bodily inequality, one wonders what could possibly be expected from Wollstonecraft in terms of a defence of women's bodily strength.

To answer this worry, we need to note that these comments and others like them do not straightforwardly convey the idea that men are naturally stronger than women. Firstly, as one writer on Wollstonecraft, Adriana Craciun, has noticed, there are always qualifiers in Wollstonecraft's concessions of men's physical superiority (Craciun 2002, 65). She adds qualifying and conditional terms, such as 'apparent inferiority' (Wollstonecraft 2014, 32–3), 'seems' (65), and an 'if' precedes the passage cited from (66). Secondly, this apparent superiority is never to be accepted silently. Nearly every time she mentions it, Wollstonecraft asks why women do not seek to improve their own strength, or why they wear their learned physical weakness as badge of femininity. Why should women, she asks, be proud of a 'defect' (66)? On the next page she starts a sentence with the words 'should it be proved that woman is naturally weaker than man' (67), suggesting that it is not, in fact, certain that they are.

What does Wollstonecraft conclude from this observed difference in bodily strength in men and women? One of her central claims is that upper- and middle-class women are forced, through education, to weaken their bodies, while men of the same classes are allowed to strengthen theirs. This, she says, is part of a gendered system of education that condemns little girls to live a 'sedentary life' which 'weakens the muscles and releases the nerves' while 'boys frolic in the open air' (Wollstonecraft 2014, 68). That sedentary life involves sitting for hours listening to their nurse's gossip, or watching their mother dress and apply make-up, or playing with a doll, or making pretty clothes to impress female relatives. However, Wollstonecraft argues, girls left to themselves will not play with dolls, but will want to 'romp' in the same way as boys do. This is something she believes to be true of all animals, human animals included: in order to grow strong and healthy, young animals play and exercise their bodies (68).

Outdoor play and exercise is not merely useful for building muscle: the mind also needs the support of the body in order to grow. Wollstonecraft had no time for the myth of the sickly genius. She cites the natural philosopher Joseph Priestley who wrote that 'the majority of great men have lived beyond forty-five' (Wollstonecraft 2014, 65).[1] In line with this observation, she notes that women who strike her as rational often turn out to be healthier than other women in their class. The rational women she knows, she says, are nearly all women who have 'accidentally been allowed to run wild' during their childhood (69), that is, women who have escaped the 'constant

---

[1] This means that geniuses lived to be older than average. Until the late nineteenth century, average life expectancy stayed below forty-five in the UK (UN Desa and Gapminder 2019).

attention of a nurse' (68) and did not, therefore, become 'enervated by confinement' (49).

The claim that women's health, whether physical or psychological, is harmed by not benefiting from free outdoor play as children is one that still attracts the attention of researchers. In 2011, philosopher of science Sharyn Clough published a paper on a known correlation in North-Western industrialized countries between increased hygiene and increased incidence of allergies, asthma, and auto-immune disorders. The less children are exposed to dirt, the more likely they are to develop these diseases. Having noted that women were 'over-represented in these clinical populations', Clough decided to ask whether feminist thought and methodology might help understand why. So she asked what hygienic differences there were in early childhood (when they are most relevant) between boys and girls. And she came up with all the points that Wollstonecraft makes in the *Rights of Woman*.

Clough's argument is as follows. Girls, for a number of reasons, play less in the dirt than boys do. Playing in the dirt is a good way to protect oneself against allergies, asthma, and auto-immune disorders (this is the Hygiene Hypothesis). Therefore, girls are less well protected against these diseases than boys. It is her defence of the first premise that brings feminist methodology to the argument. Clough cites a number of studies to the effect that girls are less likely to play outdoors unsupervised. A few of her facts are as follows:

(1) Girls are more likely to wear clothes that are not supposed to get dirty (all those cute dresses are dry clean only!).
(2) Girls' clothes are more confining, therefore harder to play rough in.
(3) Girls are constantly monitoring their decorum, and climbing or tumbling in a dress often means letting one's knickers show.
(4) Girls' leisure activities are more likely to be closely monitored.
(5) Girls' leisure activities are more likely to be organized indoors.

It is striking that this very recent argument, despite its reliance on modern medical knowledge (and dry cleaning), basically reiterates what Mary Wollstonecraft told us over two centuries ago. Girls can't play rough because they are under 'the constant attention of a nurse'. They are encouraged to play indoors – a 'sedentary life, sitting for hours' – and to make their clothes prettier to impress female relatives. Does this mean that Wollstonecraft's findings should be regarded as scientific? Or were they just a lucky guess? To the extent that Wollstonecraft refers to her experience as a teacher of girls and an observer of childhood, we should consider her observations to be indicative of the need to conduct research. Social sciences methods did not come into being till much later, so we cannot hold Wollstonecraft's views to their standards. But we can treat her observations as those of an acute observer who is willing to look beyond social prejudice in order to study childhood.

It is, also, amazing that things should have changed so little, but also that they should still need pointing out. Of course, this is not the only instance of a historical philosopher making a claim that we keep on rediscovering and not acting on. In the early years of the fifteenth century, philosopher Christine de Pisan argued that a woman choosing to wear nice clothes was not, in any way, a sign that she wanted to be sexually assaulted (or even that she was sexually available) – a truth that many men, women, police officers, and judges still find difficult to grasp today. But why forget? Why not ensure that these facts are remembered, by teaching authors such as Pisan and Wollstonecraft in schools, breaking with the often exclusively male curriculum of history, literature, and philosophy?

Throwing like a Confident Mediocre White Man – Gender beyond the Body

One way a person might read Wollstonecraft's claims about the realities of women's mis-education and the negative effect on their health is that these things happen as the result of ignorance. Kindergarten teachers, and parents of young children, genuinely believe that it is right and proper to treat boys and girls differently, and once it is pointed out to them clearly and convincingly that they are harming their children, they will change their minds. This attitude is usually cashed out in a strong trust in educational reforms: gender equality is an attitude that can be taught by delivering the right kind of material, but also, as Wollstonecraft herself insists, by teaching girls and boys together, thereby ensuring that they learn first to know, and hopefully respect, each other from an early age (Wollstonecraft 2014, 198–9). To some extent this is also the claim behind Clough's paper: if only parents knew that by letting their daughter wear that pretty dress which they were given by a favourite aunt to school they would increase their risk of disease later on, they would probably put their foot down. And if they knew that by insisting girls keep their legs together when sitting, and not make their knickers visible by bending down, and so on, they were doing the same thing, surely (hopefully) they (some of them) would try to stop.

But would that be enough? How many little girls have learnt to keep their knickers from showing not because their parents told them to but because they were laughed at by their peers? How many right-thinking parents have been mortified to find that their little boy was mocking a girl in school because she got to the top of the climbing frame wearing a skirt? And how many feminist mothers have been disappointed that their daughter would insist on wearing girly clothes to school, despite all the fun, comfortable, and gender-neutral alternatives they bought? The temptation, as a parent or a teacher, is often to throw up one's arms in despair and admit that there may be something natural at play in gender distinctions after all.

Trust in education is bound to lead to disappointment if it's all that we rely on to bring about gender equality. Education demonstrably fails, as parents who've tried everything – 'We've never showed them gender distinctions at home, we've never encouraged girliness or boyishness, and the school we've picked is very progressive. What else can we do?' – will know. And this is so even when we consider education, the best there is, in the home as well as in schools, as recommended by Wollstonecraft, who wanted every child to attend day school so they could benefit from what the home environment had to teach.

Wollstonecraft did not live long enough to see whether educational measures based on her ideas would make a difference. But she knew that falling through the bars of accepted educational practices for girls made a difference: she had benefited from parental neglect, and, as she mentioned, other women who turned out to be reasonable had also been 'allowed to run wild' (Wollstonecraft 2014, 69). This would provide sufficient evidence, perhaps, that mis-education is to blame for women's poor health, poor morals, and reasoning skills – subtract adult interference, and girls will grow into healthy, sensible women. Yet that cannot be the answer either: children need guidance, if only to stay out of danger. But also, how do these sensible women fare in society? Are they appreciated by adults who have learned to expect something very different from women? If they become – as one might surmise – outcasts, then their influence on future generations will be limited, and their numbers will not increase. Accidental neglect, therefore, is not key to feminist progress.

Despite an immense trust in educational reform – she did, after all, dedicate the *Rights of Woman* to the Marquis de Talleyrand, because he had been put in charge of reforming the French educational system – Wollstonecraft did not confine her hopes in those reforms. She believed that what needed to be reformed was something far more nebulous and insidious: manners. Little boys pointing and laughing at a girl's exposed underwear, when their parents have taught them nothing of the sort, is a subset of 'manners', that is, those that reproduce sexist attitudes from one generation to the next. It is not transmitted overtly by a teacher or a parent, as morals sometimes are ('it's wrong to lie'), but it is nonetheless omnipresent in human societies. It is depicted in cartoons, songs, or stories for children, acted out in schoolyard games, and often present in jokes – intentionally or not – and polite behaviour, such as holding the door open for a lady. These are the manners that Wollstonecraft targeted in the late eighteenth century. Now we also have to contend with 'manners' brought to us by the world of internet and mobile phone, music videos, Pornhub, and the fast sharing of gossip on social media.

The surrounding world of 'manners', then, if we choose to call it that, is what we have to contend with over and above education, as Wollstonecraft herself was well aware:

> Men and women must be educated, in a great degree, by the opinions and manners of the society they live in. In every age there has been a stream of popular opinion that has carried all before it, and given a family character, as it were, to the century. It may then fairly be inferred, that, till society be differently constituted, much cannot be expected from education. (Wollstonecraft 2014, 47)

It is what constitutes our universe, much more than the experience of learning, at home or at school. And it is what parents fail to see when they ask: what more could I have done to prevent my child from falling under the influence of gender stereotypes? The phenomenology of sexism and bodily perception is what Iris Young tried to explain in her famous 1977 piece 'Throwing Like a Girl'. She argued that in order to understand the otherwise inexplicable gender differences we see in everyday life, we need to refer to the lived experience and 'situation' of girls and boys and the way their relationship with their own bodies develops. Boys learn to see their bodies as the originator of movement, they learn to take up space, and to use every part of their body when they move. Girls learn that their body is an object that is often targeted, can cause them pain, and should be kept close and out of the way. The source of women's tendency to 'throw like girls', to fail to develop strong and healthy bodies is, Young tells us, 'in the particular situation of women as conditioned by their sexist oppression in contemporary society' (Young 1990, 152).

Young doesn't offer any solution in this paper (though of course she went on to write much more) apart from the suggested ending of sexist oppression – which translates, I think, to Wollstonecraft's revolution in female manners – which would restore to women their lost dignity 'and make them, as a part of the human species, labour by reforming themselves to reform the world' (Wollstonecraft 2014, 71).

Young points out the quasi-universal nature – at least in the industrialized North – of women's learned bodily impairment. As a young teen, she tells us, she was practising how to 'walk like a woman', with small, stiff steps, in contrast to the bigger and freer stride of men (Young 1990, 153). But Wollstonecraft is not as convinced as Young seems to be that this experience is inevitable. She is, after all, able to criticize the underdeveloped muscles of aristocratic women from an aesthetic perspective, claiming that 'the body is prevented from attaining that grace and beauty which relaxed, half-formed limbs never exhibit' (Wollstonecraft 2014, 49). Not only does Wollstonecraft speak out against this unnatural aesthetic but she also tells us that some women she knows (and indeed herself) have escaped this 'deplorable fate' of being made to live in a weak body, that the mind 'shapes itself' like a bird that, 'roaming round its gilded cage, only seeks to adorn its prison' (Wollstonecraft 2014, 70).

Wollstonecraft's perspective, therefore, is not quite that of Young, who by studying the 'situation' of women in the industrialized North-West gives substance to what parents' experience when they throw up their arms and say there is nothing they can do to fight the tide of gender stereotypes. Wollstonecraft knows it can be fought, and knows it is not inevitable. There are, after all, examples of women who have escaped this tide.

One of these women, whose name she gives at the beginning of chapter 5, is Madame d'Eon. Madame d'Eon, whom we might now call a trans woman, started her life as a woman in her forties. She dressed as a woman, but reluctantly and only partially, as she did not find feminine accoutrement to be comfortable or convenient for her preferred activity – fencing. Madame D'Eon was a celebrated swordswoman, performing duels for money in London when she had run out of other financial support. This alone might explain why Madame d'Eon was considered a role model by Wollstonecraft. Brought up as a man, offered all the physical education necessary for a military career, Madame d'Eon was certainly a healthy individual, one who was not impaired by weak, underdeveloped muscles, or the lack of confidence to move her body. As the Chevalier d'Eon, she had been physically unexceptional (although clearly very good at using her body as she was a renowned sword fighter), because she was quite short. As Madame d'Eon, she was remarkable. Note that I am not saying here that she had a physical advantage over women because she was – perhaps – biologically male. What matters here is that Madame d'Eon was brought up as a boy, not a girl, so that her body had the chance to develop properly, and so as a woman she differed from her peers not because of her natural strength but because her body had not been inhibited in its development by 'female manners'.

Wollstonecraft's less quasi-universalist approach also enables her to be more inclusive. Young warns her readers at the beginning of her paper that she is only going to talk about 'women in contemporary advanced, industrial, urban and commercial societies' (Young 1990, 140). But even so her discussion seems a little exclusive in the way that Betty Friedan's was in *The Feminine Mystique* (1963). Industrialized urban commercial societies are not composed uniquely of middle-class white people, with women seeking above all to conform to certain bodily expectations. In the world Young talks about, toilets still needed to be cleaned, and the body of a woman who cleans them for a living is going to be different from that of a woman who belongs to the middle or upper classes. Their gait will not resemble that of a woman working in an office, or one who stays at home. It will be heavy and tired, not light and elegant. Her arms will be muscular – like those of Sojourner Truth, who enjoined the Akron, Ohio Women's Convention participants to 'Look at my arm! I have ploughed and planted, and gathered into barns, and no man could head me!'[2] Young could add that these women's 'situation' is a different one. But that would not capture everything about them. They too, like Sojourner Truth, are women. They too are the subject of male oppression in those very societies Young is commenting on. But as Wollstonecraft says, women of different classes are oppressed differently. Men make slaves of them for different purposes.

The way in which some women's condition is highlighted, while others' is obscured, even while we are trying to protect women from oppression, is perfectly illustrated by Margaret Atwood's feminist dystopia *The Handmaid's Tale*, in which women are divided up according to class and dressed in different colours, depending on whether they are to serve as Handmaids (women who bear children for rich couples), Wives (who stay home and direct the education of the children), Aunts (educators who ensure that women do not step out of their place), Marthas (servants), Econowives (labourers), or Unwomen (disruptive individuals who get sent to the colonies). What Atwood makes very clear is that only a very small proportion of the female population conform to the professed ideals – in this case of domesticated, dignified motherhood and subservient wifehood – and that the role of the rest of the women is to make sure that the framework needed for their performance remains in place. But what is projected is the performance, the rest happens in the background – behind the scenes – and so we might be excused for thinking that this is all there is, and that womanhood is exactly what is being displayed by this minority of women.

Wollstonecraft, I believe, was aware of this optical illusion that society plays on us. This is why she does not address aristocratic women but only middle-class ones, who might aspire to the ideal of

---

[2] Sojourner Truth's 1851 Akron speech is reprinted in Dawson 2023, 42–3.

the aristocratic woman but don't quite have the material means to pull it off. But she is aware that the lure of the feminine body and of aristocratic manners is going to influence women from those classes that have enough leisure to want to copy them. And this is probably what she understands by 'fashion':

> An air of fashion, which is but a badge of slavery, and proves that the soul has not a strong individual character, awes simple country people into an imitation of the vices, when they cannot catch the slippery graces, of politeness. (Wollstonecraft 2014, 42)

Wollstonecraft's division between 'manners', which are transmitted by society at large and supported by its institution, and 'morals', which can be taught in good schools and good homes – and her observation that while the two ought to be the same but in fact are not – leaves some room for hope. She still believes that 'feminine weakness' is hard to fight, and that it depends on more than education and the values of parents, but she has identified something a bit more tangible than Young's 'situation'. There is at least a sense in which women can escape the tyranny of manners to become strong and healthy, and some hope that education will eventually help defeat harmful manners.

The Parental – Mostly Maternal – Body as a Tool for Educating Children

'Historically, within the field of philosophy, birth, natality and the maternal have featured and functioned far more as metaphor than as concrete, embodied, lived experiences of birth, care and maternal relations.' This remark opens a paper by feminist philosopher Charlotte Knowles on the question of the maternal in philosophy (Knowles 2020, 17). Not many philosophers before the twentieth century, even feminist philosophers, have written about the experience of pregnancy, giving birth, breastfeeding, or any other phenomenon associated with motherhood. Wollstonecraft does not shy away from these topics. But whereas other philosophers, by failing to consider them, minimize (to the point of invisibility) this part of the human (woman) experience, one might worry that Wollstonecraft makes it too big a part of it.

Wollstonecraft seems at times to be condemning women to their maternal duties, to the extent that she claims that a mother who does not fulfil hers does not deserve the title of citizen (Wollstonecraft 2014, 176), but it is important to point out that she does not: women, she says, ought to have other avenues open to them besides marriage and motherhood. They ought to be able to find fulfilment in their careers, in intellectual or artistic pursuits (177). But her attitude is nonetheless quite far from what we would call modern. Without effective contraception and safe or legal abortion marriage – or even taking a lover, as Wollstonecraft found out, twice – was likely to mean motherhood. It followed that motherhood was, after all, women's 'grand destination' (90).

Was Wollstonecraft then making empty promises when she told women they could find fulfilment outside of marriage and motherhood? No: many women could not marry because they did not have sufficient money or were never introduced to a man likely to offer marriage. And while Wollstonecraft herself lived through two wanted pregnancies that happened outside of marriage, this was not a practice that most women would have dared to embrace. In that sense, choosing not to marry could mean choosing to remain childless.

Another way in which Wollstonecraft was making space in women's lives for pursuits other than motherhood was by condemning the practice of early marriage – until, at least, the educational system was reformed and made equal for boys and girls (Wollstonecraft 2014, 200) – because it prevented women from acquiring the experience that would enable them to make good choices and, in turn, to become good mothers. This is carefully explained in *Thoughts on the Education of Daughters*, where she says that girls go straight from the nursery of their father's home to that of their children, becoming mothers before they get the chance to grow up and to learn something about the world and about themselves (1989, vol 4, 31). What Wollstonecraft is offering women is the choice not to be child-brides, but to grow and find a place in the world for themselves, and only to marry (and probably become parents) if they choose to and if they meet a person who will do as a husband. So while motherhood on Wollstonecraft's picture is still bound to be the fate of a large proportion of women, it is, in many respects, more of a choice.

Women will probably be mothers. And as mothers, they will be called upon to feed and care for an infant, and make sure they grow up to be thoughtful, kind, and dutiful adults. The latter part of that job can, and according to Wollstonecraft should, be shared. Men have as much of a duty to be good fathers as women have to be good mothers. Setting an example by leading a virtuous life themselves, engaging children in educational activities that will help them develop their minds and bodies, can be done by a father as much as it can by a mother. And this is the picture of parenting a toddler which Wollstonecraft gives us in the unfinished and unpublished book *Lessons for Children* which she wrote for her older daughter Fanny when she was pregnant with Mary. In her book, the education of the child is divided up between the parents, as is her care. If Mama has a headache, then it is Papa who teaches her that she must be quiet (1989, vol 4, 473–4). And if Papa is sleeping, she quietly asks Mama to 'Pray reach me my ball' so that she may play outside (474). Papa and Mama care for each other in this way because they love each other, and because they are wise enough to know what is needed in such cases. The knowledge and the work of everyday care is divided between the mother and father, it seems (to some extent, anyway). But all this comes after the first two years of a child's life. Before, and again nine months before that, the burden is mostly borne by the mother.

We need to take a historical step back before going any further. The possibilities in the eighteenth century for raising a baby were rather different from what they are now. Formula milk did not exist, nor did bottles with rubber teats. A child who could not be breastfed would most often die. Babies in orphanages were fed with a sponge dipped in a mixture of cow's milk and broth. Unsurprisingly, very few survived on such a diet. This did not mean that women were obliged to breastfeed their own babies. For some women the practice of wet-nursing was available. A wet-nurse was a lactating woman who was paid to feed other people's children. She would most often take the child to live with her for the first two years of their life, with the parents visiting when they chose.

One advantage of sending one's child out to a wet-nurse would be a healthier environment. Some Parisian middle-class women at the time Wollstonecraft wrote would send their babies out to live with a nurse in the countryside, giving them a better chance of surviving their first two years. This was the case with Manon Roland's mother, who, having lost her previous babies, decided to send her daughter out to a wet-nurse. While Manon Roland herself chose to feed her own daughter, she seemed to think her mother made the right decision. But the practice differed greatly depending on the social class of the parents. In France, generally, the practice of sending children out to wet-nurses was also sometimes the result of economic necessity: women who worked could not take time off to care for babies.[3]

The women Wollstonecraft criticizes very sternly for not feeding their own babies were aristocratic women, who did not want a breastfeeding baby interfering with their social lives – or whose husbands did not want it. The aristocratic baby was sent out to live in a nearby cottage, and more or less forgotten about until they were big enough, if they were a boy, to be sent out to school.[4] This was the sort of parenting failure she decried when she said that a mother who did not care for her child did not deserve to be a citizen. One may sympathize with Wollstonecraft – but also with those mothers who may, after all, have had very little choice as to whether they could keep their babies with them. Thérèse Levasseur, Rousseau's partner, begged to be allowed to keep at least one of the children who was born from their union, but Rousseau, who felt that a family would cramp his style, refused, and had all their babies sent to an orphanage.

Did Wollstonecraft attempt to put some of the responsibility of early childhood on men's shoulders? Yes, in so far as she criticized aristocratic men for preventing their wives from breastfeeding their children so that they only 'dress and live to please them' (100). In a sense it does place a bodily restriction on husbands to prevent them from keeping their wives' bodies exclusively as their playthings, but that seems much lighter a duty than actually having to use one's body to sustain a child, whether before or after its birth. It seems that she was inclined, as far as her

---

[3] See Mary Jacobus (1992) for a discussion of wet-nursing during the French Revolution.

[4] Again, this was not universal. In France, Madame Necker, a great fan of Rousseau who argued in *Emile* in favour of mothers feeding their own babies, tried and failed to feed her daughter (Germaine de Staël). After battling with depression she decided to enlist the help of a wet-nurse, but she had her live in their home, and spent much of her time with her daughter, even though she could not feed her. See Gutwirth (2004, 19–20).

medical knowledge allowed, to put some of the responsibility for the child's growth on the father's physical (and moral) health:

> The father of a family will not then weaken his constitution and debase his sentiments, by visiting the harlot, nor forget, in obeying the call of appetite, the purpose for which it was implanted. (2014, 24 (Dedication))

This very brief passage is no doubt a reference to syphilis, which would not only weaken the father's constitution, preventing him from looking after his family, but also quite likely affect the health of his wife and children.[5] Syphilis was a significant social scourge that affected not only the prostitutes who transmitted it and the men who caught it from them but also these men's wives and their children. Men would pass on syphilis to their wives, sometimes not even knowing they had it (as the symptoms are not constant), and a woman who had contracted syphilis would pass it on to her children in the womb, resulting in miscarriage, infant death, or sickly children who did not live long.[6] In this context, other passages stand out in the *Rights of Woman*. In chapter 8, she talks of 'the rich sensualist, who has rioted among women, spreading depravity and misery, when he wishes to perpetuate his name, receives from his wife only a half-formed being that inherits both its father's and mother's weakness' (2014, 168). And in chapter 12, she writes that 'it is vain to expect the present race of weak mothers either to take that reasonable care of a child's body, which is necessary to lay the foundation of a good constitution, supposing that it do not suffer for the sins of its fathers' (208). If we focus on her first novel, *Mary*, and her emphasis on modesty as chastity in her second *Vindication*, it is easy to read Wollstonecraft as a puritan who denies the importance of bodily, sexual pleasure in life, and pairs it too easily with moral decadence. But it is clear from these passages that what concerns her is the effect that men's frequenting of prostitutes has on their wives' and children's bodily health at least as much as on their morals.

---

[5] Diana Edelman-Young (2014, 689) makes a good case for the claim that not only was Wollstonecraft conversant with the effects of syphilis on families but that also her references to soldiers are designed to remind the readers of their role in the spread of syphilis through society.

[6] A recent study has shown that by the end of the eighteenth century, when Wollstonecraft was writing, at least 20 per cent of Londoners had contracted syphilis by the age of thirty-five (Szreter and Siena 2021).

The passage in which Wollstonecraft talks of the defects of children born from libertine parents (probably because they have contracted syphilis) also mentions abortion as a recourse of women who 'have not sufficient strength to discharge the first duty of a mother; and sacrificing to lasciviousness the parental affection, that ennobles instinct, either destroy the embryo in the womb, or cast it off when born' (2014, 168). While 'abortion', at the time Wollstonecraft wrote, was also used to mean 'miscarriage', and while syphilis did cause miscarriage, it is clear in this passage that she is speaking of intentionally bringing an end to a pregnancy.[7] Perhaps because abortion was an even greater taboo in eighteenth-century England than it is now, Wollstonecraft does not mention abortion elsewhere in the *Vindication*. But she does in *The Wrongs of Woman*, where Jemima tells the story of how she took a potion in order to abort after she was raped by her employer.

First, she finds that she is pregnant:

> [I] discovered, with horror -ah! what horror! -that I was with child. I know not why I felt a mixed sensation of despair and tenderness, excepting that, ever called a bastard, a bastard appeared to me an object of the greatest compassion in creation. (Wollstonecraft 1989, vol 1, 110)

The discovery is horrible, because the pregnancy is the result of rape, because it will cause Jemima to lose her job and only means of survival when it is inevitably discovered, and because if she gives birth, she will perpetuate her fate – of a poor, unwanted, illegitimate child – on her offspring. And yet she feels love towards the unborn child. Even though Jemima's situation is possibly the lowest on the scale of disadvantage, and even though very few would fail to feel compassion for her deciding she had to abort, she is portrayed as conflicted. Wollstonecraft is making the point that Rosalind Hursthouse made in her paper 'Virtue Theory and Abortion', namely that most cases of abortion are complex and bring into play conflicting emotions and a hard decision-making process (Hursthouse 1991, 239). Jemima's story as told by Wollstonecraft

---

[7] 'No qualitative difference existed between *abortion* and *miscarriage* in the discourse of the period including medical literature' (Cooper 2004, 736).

highlights the heart-wrenching steps that led to the abortion. Firstly, she decides that she will not take the potion given to her:

> After some weeks of deliberation had elapsed, I in continual fear that my altered shape would be noticed, my master gave me a medicine in a phial, which he desired me to take, telling me, without any circumlocution, for what purpose it was designed. I burst into tears, I thought it was killing myself – yet was such a self worth preserving? He cursed me for a fool, and left me to my own reflections. I could not resolve to take this infernal potion; but I wrapped it up in an old gown, and hid it in a corner of my box. (Wollstonecraft 1989, vol I, 111)

Jemima refuses the medicine because she is afraid of it – afraid what it will do to her. But yet, she is not entirely unwilling to die, and we know already that she felt some compassion for her unborn offspring. Perhaps, as Cooper suggests, Jemima is identifying here with her foetus, one unfortunate bastard with another, and reflecting on her mother's decision to keep her alive and subject her to such a miserable fate (Cooper 2004, 764–6). Then the inevitable happens: her pregnancy starts to show, and she is thrown out into the streets, blamed for her own rape and treated like a thief (111). Then new emotions take hold of her, and she decides to abort:

> I hurried back to my hole, and, rage giving place to despair, sought for the potion that was to procure abortion, and swallowed it, with a wish that it might destroy me, at the same time that it stopped the sensations of new-born life, which I felt with indescribable emotion. My head turned round, my heart grew sick, and in the horrors of approaching dissolution, mental anguish was swallowed up. The effect of the medicine was violent, and I was confined to my bed several days. (Wollstonecraft 1989, vol I, 112)

But while Jemima may have wished to die, she soon gets better and must find both a place to go and an occupation. The only opportunity available, of course, was prostitution, and out of a desire to survive she takes it up – first in the streets, then in a brothel, and finally at the home of an older man. Jemima does not mention further abortions. Perhaps her first abortion made it impossible for her to become pregnant again, and after a short while she was able to leave the streets to become the live-in mistress of an older man who presumably was no longer able to have children. But if she did not abort herself, Jemima was again scarred by the loss of an unborn child, that of her new lover's previous mistress, whom she persuaded him to kick out. The woman, pregnant and with nowhere to go, drowned herself. Jemima saved her own life at the cost of theirs.

Jemima does not seek to make excuses for herself, but she cannot then face taking up the dead woman's place and seeks other ways of keeping herself alive, until eventually she becomes Maria's jailer and tells Maria her story. The abortion, despite its deep emotional consequences and the moral deliberations and realizations it forced Jemima to engage in, did not make her a better person. It made her a poorer, sicker, and more desperate one. Her telling the story to new friends Maria and Darnford is her first opportunity to put together these experiences and reflections, and perhaps to begin to understand the effect of the abortion, among all the other acts which were forced on her by others and by her situation, and to reflect on what she might now become. Jemima's body was, as she tells it herself, enslaved. It was not her own, even when, as she says, she maintained some independence by working the streets rather than joining a brothel. But it was nonetheless hers to keep alive. And keeping herself alive was the entire focus of her life, to the extent that she was able to sacrifice a woman and her unborn child so that she could have a roof over her head.

Wollstonecraft's telling of Jemima's story puts into stark perspective the vision of the woman's body as a source of pleasure for men (and women) on the one hand, and as the centre of pain and indignity which is nonetheless one's own to protect as it is the source of life, on the other. Abortion, rather than being a moral problem of its own, is depicted within this perspective. Jemima aborts to protect herself even as she experiences the last throes of her human capacity for compassion. What could in fact have protected Jemima? A better education, so she knew how to avoid pregnancy? This is hardly likely as her pregnancy was the result of being raped by her employer. Would a better education for her employer, or her parents, or her parents' employer have made a difference? Perhaps, and Wollstonecraft is certainly hoping that a widespread reform of education and of all the institutions that perpetuate harmful and sexist manners will eventually protect women. The motive of the novel *Maria*, in which we find the portrait of Jemima, is after all 'the desire of exhibiting the misery and oppression, peculiar to women, that arise out of the partial laws and customs of society'. The fate of Jemima is determined by these partial laws and customs. No social reform will ever eradicate crime, including rape – you might say. Perhaps, but while Jemima becomes pregnant because she is raped, she becomes sick because she performs an unsafe and illegal abortion, she becomes a prostitute because the stigma of having been pregnant outside marriage prevents her from obtaining other employment, and finally she becomes the (indirect) murderer of a rival, because the life she has been forced to live wiped out any natural moral sentiment she may have had to start with, instead of nurturing it as it should have.

When Wollstonecraft writes about the body, she anticipates many of the current discussions we now have about the sexed and gendered body, about the ways in which our gendered upbringing and our gendered living affect our health. One realization we come to when reading Wollstonecraft is how little has changed since the eighteenth century. Women's health still suffers from beauty standards, and beauty standards are still used as a way to enforce patriarchy.

CHAPTER 5

Happy Families

Wollstonecraft wrote a great deal about the education of children: one short treatise, *Thoughts on the Education of Daughters*, a book for children and educators, *Original Stories for Children*, and an unfinished primer she wrote for her daughter. In all these, and in relevant sections of the *Rights of Woman*, she argued that children should be taught to use their reason, to feel appropriate emotions, and to respect each other. All of this has a strong relational element: Wollstonecraft suggests that adults should encourage children to ask questions and leave them to argue amongst themselves so as to use their reasoning more freely. Her notion of parental responsibility and childhood duties – underlying her educational programme – turns out to be just as radical as her other ideas. Wollstonecraft equates the responsibilities of mothers and fathers, and argues against the (then predominant) view of parents as having the right to do as they chose with their children, proposing some limitations to parental domination.

The Last Bastion of Tyranny

Republican philosophers such as Wollstonecraft often seek to extend their condemnation of tyranny from that of the king over the people, to the master over those they enslave, and the husband over the wife. But there is one area of human relations where one might be reluctant to interfere (and human–animal relations are another thing altogether). That is the relation between non-adult children and their carers. Children have a legal status as dependent: that is, they do not enjoy the full exercise of human rights (for instance, in many countries a child cannot vote, get married, or work for a living). Instead, they are subject to children's rights, the purpose of which is to protect them so that they can reach the age of majority in the best possible way: that is, unharmed, generally safe, educated, and ready to live independently.

But the fact that children do not enjoy the same rights as mature human beings, and the fact that they must be protected, makes them dependent on the will of older humans whose job it is to help them grow. In most cases these will be close family members or paid professionals (nursemaids and teachers) who work either for the family or for an institution. Any adult may be either the sole or the joint carer of a child. A single parent may homeschool their child, and do so in such an exclusive way that they are never cared for by anyone else. A child can be brought up in an institution where staff have full power over them (boarding schools and orphanages), or they can be cared for by a mixture of family members and professionals (i.e. they live with their parents but attend day school).

It is easy to assume that children who have fewer responsible adults in their lives are more likely to be subject to parental tyranny. Think, for instance, of Carrie's mother, in the novel and film(s) of the same name: as the adult responsible for her daughter's religious education, she attempts to break her daughter's will entirely, and as a result turns her into a killer. But while being under the exclusive care of a malevolent parent is a terrible situation to be in, it would be a mistake to think that a larger number of less tyrannical carers – be they family members, teachers, neighbours, or friends – necessarily means more freedom. In measuring a child's liberty to grow, we must also take into account the social influence of what Wollstonecraft calls 'manners'. A child brought up in a society where everyone agrees that children like them have a certain place will be just as much subject to tyranny as the child of a single and tyrannical parent. Perhaps, in fact, more: a child can escape from a parent, but it's harder to escape from a community. One extreme case of a tyrannical community would be the religious sect, but even respectable middle-class eighteenth-century England, as far as Wollstonecraft is concerned, routinely tyrannizes over daughters.

Anca Gheaus (2021) argues that contemporary republicans very rarely think about the parent–child relationship when they explore relationships of domination. Yet, she says, these relationships are paradigmatic cases of asymmetrical power, with parents dominating children, very often arbitrarily. A parent may decide that their child will not receive medical care, or that they will not be educated, or they may impose on them a religion that will shape their entire character and possibly their lives. They may do all these things simply because they are the adults in charge. The parent–child relationship is not the same everywhere in the world – some states have more of a say on what is owed to children, and some protect parental rights to make decisions more closely. But in most countries, children are exposed to their parents' whims, and that makes parental authority tyrannical.

Wollstonecraft is intent on annihilating tyranny in families and freeing children from arbitrary domination. 'Parental affection', she writes, 'is but a pretext to tyrannize when it can be done with impunity' (2014, 180). The sort of parental tyranny she has in mind, which expresses itself in forcing children to marry or to take up a particular profession they are unsuited for, is still one we observe in many parts of the world. But even families where this sort of thing does not happen – either because the culture they belong to does not require them to make that sort of decision for their children or because they are not rich and there is no inheritance to place, share, or save – there is still plenty of tyrannical behaviour to be observed. A child may be prevented from seeing a set of friends, from enjoying the same kind of activities others enjoy, from having the time and space to study for school, and even from getting enough sleep (supposing the parents argue loudly at night). All these things can happen without social services getting involved. Think, again, of Stephen King's *Carrie*. Her mother prevents her from talking to boys, which means that she cannot make friends with others in her class. Her mother chooses clothes for her, and prevents her from getting a job so she may buy new ones. She prevents her from finding out about anything related to sexuality, so that Carrie is frightened when she has her first period. Because of all this, Carrie is mocked and bullied at school, which eventually culminates in her being doused in pig's blood at the school prom.

But domination can also be benign: a child needs to be told what to do, and simply cannot make certain decisions for themselves. As Plato argues in *Crito*, obedience is a requisite for habit formation: if we do not obey our parents, we may never learn to live freely as an adult. Take the example of playing a musical instrument. To play it well – in a way that will maximize enjoyment of music later in life – it is important to start young, and to practise regularly. But very few children will choose to stay indoors and practise scales every day when they could be playing with friends or losing themselves in a book or a video game. And this goes for every area of learning: a child must be taught hygiene, must be made to brush their teeth, wash their hands, and so on, otherwise their health will suffer and their life may even be shortened. And although not all children do best in school, and not all children learn in the same way, some attempt must be made at finding them a good programme of education and helping them to stick with it. Allowing children to stay out of school on a whim – not insisting on their doing homework they have been given, that they are capable of doing, and have time and space to do – is to wrong them. Even if this 'insisting' takes the form of soft persuasion – such as promising treats when homework is completed or gently reasoning with the child that they can do their other activities at some later time – this is still in an important sense a form of domination. Parents know that they will in the end have the final word, and that they must, for the good of the child. If they do not dominate, they are failing their child.

This is what Anca Gheaus means when she writes that '[d]omination cannot be fully eliminated from child-rearing without unacceptable loss of value. Most likely, republicanism requires that we minimize children's domination' (2021, 748). How do we do this? And how does Wollstonecraft, who genuinely wants to erase domination from every kind of human relation, suggest we do it?

To go back to our musical education example, not every child should play the piano, and a child who is not naturally inclined to an instrument may find its practice very punitive, and this may lower their self-esteem. A teacher experienced in teaching music may help a child discover an aptitude, in which case it may be worth encouraging the child to practise, but a parent is less likely to have the opportunity to experience various instruments and more likely to project their own ambitions on a child. So even in the case of something as benign as musical education, parental domination can be harmful. This is because they are not necessarily equipped to make the best, least harmful decisions for their children. They may be in the best place to enforce them, because they have most control over the child's time and living space, but this just means that bad parental judgement quickly becomes tyrannical. A child who is homeschooled (unless as part of a community of homeschooling) is quickly isolated not only from their peers but also from other human beings, and even a simple punishment, such as grounding, adds to this isolation. Their entire world is parental rule and they have no refuge from it.

Wollstonecraft's solution to this sort of familial tyranny is to make sure that the child has more qualified adults in their lives. Firstly, she believes that education should be conducted in day schools, ensuring children have two separate spheres in which they can learn and grow, and at the same time, though she does not say it, an escape from each. School, she says, is where children will learn to develop their reasoning skills, and they will do so not just by sitting in classrooms and listening to teachers, but by arguing with their peers during free time, at the same time as they get fresh air and exercise. Home is where they will learn how to develop healthy emotions, how to bond with those they love, and how to be happy. Again, this can only happen if parents have their child's best interests at heart, and if they have been educated in a way that will enable them to understand what those best interests are and how to further them. All this is rather tenuous: does Wollstonecraft imagine a time will come when all parents will be educated, but also sufficiently kind and patient and in control of their emotions to think of their child first, and always treat them in a way that will not harm them? This is a lot to ask of parents who are trying to live their own lives as best they can and earn enough so they can bring up their children. The best parents will occasionally snap, because they are tired, because they are worried, or because children are routinely trying to the most patient of individuals. The same goes for teachers – enlightened domination is too much to ask of anyone. So, what else does Wollstonecraft propose? It seems her view is that the role of educators, parental or outsiders, is to shorten the time when a child will be dominated, by helping them acquire what is needed to balance the power in a relationship, which is reason.

Wollstonecraft is in agreement with Gheaus that the exclusive parent–child relationship is, by nature, incapable of yielding good results:

> The good effects resulting from attention to private education will ever be very confined, and the parent who really puts his own hand to the

plow, will always, in some degree, be disappointed, till education becomes a grand national concern. (Wollstonecraft 2014, 188)

The reason is twofold. Firstly, the parent cannot take the child to a desert and do what they will with it. Even if the parent makes their best effort, the rest of the world will also have an input into the education of the child. Humans are by nature social, and that means that we shape each other through our interactions with each other. Secondly, Wollstonecraft says that a parent cannot fulfil the role of the peer in the development of their child. A child's development, she says, requires playful interaction with other children. The exclusive company of adults will both stop natural impulses, because no matter how much we love a parent, there will always be some fear mixed in, and cause premature adulthood, a kind of fake maturity which bypasses all necessary stages in the child's development.[1] The two faculties that suffer most from this sort of upbringing, she says, are curiosity and critical thinking. A child brought up among adults only will lose the incentive to investigate for themselves how things work, as they know that they can get the answer simply by asking. Conversely, they will learn always to trust the answer they get, and not seek to prove or disprove it using their own reasoning skills.

Private schools, Wollstonecraft also argues, are not the solution. She has witnessed enough harm, she says, done to children's moral characters when they live amongst schoolmasters and peers, and never see their parents. They become gluttons, liars, and sexually promiscuous (2014, 189).

Wollstonecraft offers two solutions which she expects to work jointly to remedy the ills of home education and private boarding schools: children should go to day schools run by the state. That the state runs them will mean that children are guaranteed the sort of attention that doesn't kowtow to the parent. If masters are paid by the state, teachers don't need to demonstrate to parents that their child is doing well when they're not. They can afford to be more honest in their evaluation of children's progress, and hence more effective in their teaching. This is the first benefit of state-run day schools. The second is the fact that children go home to their parents in the evening, and so escape the

---

[1] Wollstonecraft seems to anticipate theories such as Piaget's, which state that we develop in a common manner, and have to go through a number of stages before reaching maturity.

constant company of their peers, which, while it will encourage critical thinking, does not offer the best moral example. In order to become emotionally and morally healthy individuals, children must be brought up in a family home:

> Few, I believe, have had much affection for mankind, who did not first love their parents, their brothers, sisters, and even the domestic brutes, whom they first played with. The exercise of youthful sympathies forms the moral temperature; and it is the recollection of these first affections and pursuits that gives life to those that are afterwards more under the direction of reason. (2014, 193)

The Age of Reason

The parent–child relationship necessarily involves some degree of domination from the very start. Parents, at least sometimes, choose to have a child, but a child never chooses to be born. Even if childbirth was almost always inevitable given the unreliability of contraception and abortion, adults would not have to become parents, but could abandon their children to an orphanage, as Rousseau did several times. But whatever an adult who finds themselves with an infant decides to do, the infant will be stuck with it (Gheaus 2021, 2). An infant also must depend wholly on their carer, as they cannot feed themselves. They lack the motor skills to move towards a source of food, unless it is placed by their mouth. And while other animals achieve autonomy more quickly, human children are relatively slow, and so must remain dependents for several years.

Wollstonecraft's proposal that children be educated in state-run day schools goes quite some way towards mitigating the exclusive domination of parents over children while they are at school. But Wollstonecraft points out that tyrannical dependence carries on much longer than the years a child may attend school, and well into the time when they could make decisions that will affect the rest of their lives, such as choosing a job or a husband or wife:

> [T]o subjugate a rational being to the mere will of another, after he is of age to answer to society for his own conduct, is a most cruel and undue stretch of power; and, perhaps, as injurious to morality as those religious

systems which do not allow right and wrong to have any existence, but in the Divine will. (Wollstonecraft 2014, 183)

But this cruel subjugation, she adds, is made possible by years of tyrannizing over children. Domination is habit forming; it shapes the mind to obey instead of thinking for itself: 'A slavish bondage to parents cramps every faculty of the mind.' Children are prepared in their childhood to obey parents in later life. This is particularly true of daughters, for whom parental tyranny is training for 'the slavery of marriage' (2014, 185). And even if domination does not turn children into slaves, they may still end up bound to their parents by inheritance: the threat of being 'cut off' from their inheritance is often enough of a reason, at least for the well-off, to pretend to respect and obey their parents until their death.

All this, Wollstonecraft argues, is reason for ending the practice of parenting as domination as quickly as possible. Parents may be required to impose their will on infants, but they should stop doing so as soon as possible, and remember that this is a reciprocal duty: as they observe their duty of care towards 'helpless infancy', they can expect to be cared for when 'the feebleness of age' comes upon them (2014, 183). This should be (but often isn't) a good way to limit tyrannical behaviour. If one is relying on one's children in old age, one had better help them grow into kind and responsible adults. A carer with years of grudges is not what we want when we can no longer care for ourselves.

The best practice, then, must be to accept that a certain amount of caring domination is called for early on in a child's life, but that it should stop as soon as possible. When, then, do children stop being candidates for domination? As far as Wollstonecraft is concerned, this happens progressively, and starts very early on: it is linked to children's developing their reasoning skills. Provided that children are encouraged to develop their reason – which, we saw, can only happen when they are allowed to study among their peers – they become less helpless and develop the means to redress the fundamental imbalance they are born with. Thus, arbitrariness diminishes as children grow in reason and are able to argue against what they think is wrong, and accept what they are persuaded to do is right. And if parents actively encourage children's reasoning skills, then they are helping them move away from the phase of their lives when they must be dominated.

This does not entail that children should stop obeying their parents. They still need to be protected by their parents; hence they must obey. But they must do it rationally – in the understanding that they can ask questions (later if needed) and that they can engage their parents in debates as to whether they made the right call in telling them what to do. In order to minimize domination, then, this must happen as soon as children are capable of reasoning, and that, according to Wollstonecraft, can happen quite early. 'Children cannot be taught too early to submit to reason' – she says in the second *Vindication*. But parents should also make it explicit to children that this progress is happening, and that soon they will not need to obey their parents: 'your reason is now gaining strength, and till it arrives at some degree of maturity, you must look up to me for advice – then you ought to think, and only rely on God' (Wollstonecraft 2014, 46).

One might be tempted to argue back that until she has children of her own, she should refrain from telling parents how to discipline and teach their children. It's all very well to say that a child can reason, but having to answer endless 'why' questions when one needs to leave for the school run and the child still isn't dressed is a different matter. Wollstonecraft, however, would respond that she did become a parent, and did test her hypothesis for her first daughter, Fanny. In *Lessons*, a book which she wrote for her daughter and which was published posthumously and unfinished, she engages in dialogues with her very young daughter and shows her (and us) that she can reason already.

> You say that you do not know how to think. Yes; you do a little. The other day papa was tired; he had been walking about all the morning. After dinner he fell asleep on the sopha. I did not bid you be quiet; but you thought of what papa said to you, when my head ached. This made you think that you ought not to make a noise, when papa was resting himself. So you came to me, and said to me, very softly, Pray reach me my ball, and I will go and play in the garden, till papa wakes. (1989, vol 4, 474)[2]

---

[2] It is sad and unfortunate that Fanny and Mary lost their mother so early, and that when their (step-)father, Godwin, remarried, it was to a woman prone to arbitrary domination of her stepdaughters.

If a three-year-old can begin to reason, she need not be blindly obedient. Even though she may be required to obey without arguing, she has the capacity to ask, later, why she was made to comply with her parent's wish, what it was about it that was good and meant it had to be done. What Wollstonecraft is modelling in *Lessons* is not just a child's progress but also a parent's attitude. Good parenting, as she says in the *Vindication*, is about endeavouring to give children the tools they need to come out, progressively and as soon as possible, of a relationship in which they must be dominated for their own good, and to build a more equal relationship with their parents. This has the added benefit that children brought up in this way will not in turn tyrannize others in adulthood.

The Fool and the Scarecrow: Gendered Parenting Roles

In her chapter on parental affection Wollstonecraft reminds her readers that 'the care of children in their infancy is one of the grand duties annexed to the female character by nature' (Wollstonecraft 2014, 181). This is something that has come up several times before in the *Vindication*, and, as we saw in the previous chapter, this grand duty included breastfeeding babies until they could safely be weaned. While this is problematic, it is also very much contingent on the fact that children who were not breastfed tended to die – as there was no safe alternative – and that the practice of wet-nursing in Britain in the eighteenth century mostly meant the rich sending their children away for two years to be cared for by the poor, which was not only exploitative but also resulted in poor child–parent relationships. One can well imagine that had Wollstonecraft been presented with a bottle and powdered milk, she would have been enthusiastic about parents sharing the work of caring for infants between them. In fact, one thing that is distinctive about Wollstonecraft is that although she assigns special duties to mothers for the period of infanthood, she otherwise seems to think that mothers and fathers have equal responsibilities towards the upbringing of their children.

For the first two years of her daughter's life, Wollstonecraft was – more or less – a single parent. She knew well what it meant to take on the burden of raising a child, with little help – she had one servant – and a job to do, she was still writing for a living. But once she and Godwin became a couple, and he took on the role of Fanny's father, she seems to have had the sort of life that most women still dream of: shared and equal parenting. Of course, we know very little of what their life was like, and it only lasted for a few months before Wollstonecraft died. And we also know that Godwin married again in order to have another woman care for his daughters. But the book *Lessons*, which Wollstonecraft wrote for her daughter, draws a touching picture of shared and equal parenting. Lesson X asks Fanny to recall what happened when either of her parents was sick and resting. When her mother had a headache, her father taught her not to make a noise, and showed her through example. When her father had a stomach ache, her mother made him chamomile tea. These are things they did, she tells Fanny, because they loved each other. The lesson is about love. But it's also about shared care: Papa does not ignore Fanny when Mama is ill, he takes care of her, makes sure she learns to be quiet. Fanny can call on her father and knows that he will dispense as good care and advice as her mother.

Such shared parenting, however, was no more the norm in the eighteenth century than it is now (and probably considerably less so). And much of what Wollstonecraft has to say about parenting in the second *Vindication* denounces the inequality of mothers and fathers. Indeed, the opening pages of the *Vindication*, the dedication to Talleyrand, argue that women's condition and women's virtue cannot be improved unless men, and in particular fathers, also change. Women are essential to society because they teach children. The same could be said of fathers, but in this particular argument it seems less relevant. Women are put in a situation where they must educate children, without being themselves educated. Men may and definitely should have a share of this all-important task, but they at least are somewhat prepared for it – better prepared, ironically, than women, to whom the lion's share of child care falls. But men, however well educated, are not entirely well-fitted for fatherhood either. They are prone to vice or to libertinage, which, as we saw in the previous chapter, does not only take them away from the family home, where they are needed, but also physically weakens the family by bringing home sexually transmitted diseases which they pass on to their wives, and through them to their children. So men, Wollstonecraft argues, should stay home in order to strengthen the family, both emotionally and physically. She concludes that we must ask men to be good fathers before we can ask women to be good mothers: 'till men become attentive to the duty of a father, it is vain to expect women to spend that time in the nursery which they [...] choose to spend at their glass' (Wollstonecraft 2014, 24).

The need for more equality between mother and father comes up again in the chapter on parenting, but this time to bemoan the fact that in most families mothers are regarded as indulgent while fathers are feared:

> To be a good mother – a woman must have sense, and that independence of mind which few women possess who are taught to depend entirely on their husbands. Meek wives are, in general, foolish mothers; wanting their children to love them best, and take their part, in secret, against the father, who is held up as a scarecrow. (2014, 181)

This sort of good cop/bad cop routine, she says, does not lead to anything good as far as the children or the family are concerned. Children learn to fear one parent and to abuse the other: there is no room left for respect – as Wollstonecraft is of the opinion that respect that comes from fear is not truly respect, and disappears as soon as the object of fear is removed – but also, and more importantly, there is no room for character development. A clever child will know to ask for what she wants while her father is away, and keep to herself when he is home. Lessons, which are typically conducted during the daytime when the father is out conducting business, will be skipped. Early meals before the father comes home will consist of sweets and no vegetables, disobedience and rudeness will go unpunished except at the weekend, where a clever child might learn to keep quiet for the sake of continued misbehaviour the rest of the time.

The long-term consequences are of course bad for the child, as they are for anyone who comes into contact with them once they are adults. An indulged child who simply has to avoid their father will not learn to think about whether what they want is something that will be good for them. They will just continue to make impulsive choices, and the reasoning skills that ought to go into questioning their own choices will instead be devoted to cunningly choosing when to ask.

But if mother and father were home together more, and if they spent time discussing their children's upbringing, this would not happen.

They would agree on matters such as lesson schedules, diets, and suitable behaviour. They would be unified in praising or disciplining their child. The child would not need to become cunning in order to navigate their opposite attitudes.

Good parenting, then, for Wollstonecraft, is equal parenting. Mothers and fathers need to work together to teach a child how to use their reason, but also how to be compassionate and well-behaved, so that they can become useful citizens. And she thinks that this can only be achieved if men and women receive equal education. But this does not necessarily mean that mother and father must spend equal amounts of time doing the same jobs. We have already seen that she thought it was a necessity that women do the lion's share of infant care, because they must breastfeed. She also observes that in many families it will be the man who goes to work to earn a living for his wife and children. Note that this was not the case in every family she knew: she was herself supporting not only her sisters and a younger brother through her writing but also the family of her friend Fanny Blood, after Fanny died. And Fanny's family had, before that, been supported by Fanny herself and her mother. But this was not the norm, and many young middle-class women expected that when they were married off, their husband would work to earn their keep. Women, then, would do most of the 'at-home' work, and that included looking after the children. But Wollstonecraft saw the flip side of this inequality. Breastfeeding, she says – not entirely accurately – works as contraception, so that women may ensure that they have sufficient time between births by feeding their babies for as long as possible. Moreover, children grow up and become less time-demanding. A well-organized woman might then find time to pursue her interests, be they scientific or artistic.

> And did they pursue a plan of conduct, and not waste their time in following the fashionable vagaries of dress, the management of their household and children need not shut them out from literature, or prevent their attaching themselves to a science, with that steady eye which strengthens the mind, or practising one of the fine arts that cultivate the taste. (Wollstonecraft 2014, 223)

In other words, a woman who does all her domestic and childcare work may still find time to have a life of her own provided she is well organized!

This sort of productivity advice for mothers is not all that unusual in the eighteenth century. Wollstonecraft's French Revolutionary friend Madame Roland also wrote about how a mother and wife could manage her time most efficiently so that she could still find time to do important things, like organizing a revolution (See Bergès 2022b, 87). A few years later, their American contemporary Hannah Mather Crocker argued that a woman might turn to writing once her children were all grown. Crocker had ten children, so she became a writer quite late in life: neither Wollstonecraft nor Roland lived to be forty. So perhaps her example is an argument for having fewer children, and, as Wollstonecraft recommends, doing one's best to exercise reproductive caution!

Reinventing the Wheel? Reading Rousseau's Emile as a Woman

Late eighteenth-century England was hungry for books on education, and the education of girls, in particular, was a topic that sold. Joseph Johnson, Wollstonecraft's publisher, had many such works on his list, and Wollstonecraft wrote for him not only her *Original Stories* (which he had illustrated by Blake) and *Thoughts on the Education of Daughters* but also a *Reader* for young women (Hay 2022 286). But one of the reasons for this renewed interest in education was the popularity of Rousseau's fictional memoir on education, *Emile*. Wollstonecraft, like many, had read it and had embraced most of what he had to say about the education of his fictional charge, the young Emile. The boy had started off life breastfed (ideally this would have been done by his mother, but the narrator felt that employing a healthy and biddable wet-nurse might be better in this case). And he was then encouraged to learn through experience and discovery, most of it happening outdoors, and with no adult to tell him what to think, but only his tutor, encouraging him to think for himself. This was something Wollstonecraft, along with many educational would-be reformers of the time, could get behind. In 1787, when she first read Emile, she wrote to her sister:

> I am now reading Rousseau's Emile, and love his paradoxes. He chuses a common capacity to educate – and gives as a reason that a genius will educated itself – however he rambles into that chimerical world in which

I have too often wandered – and draws the usual conclusion that all is vanity and vexation of spirit. (Wollstonecraft 1979, 145)

In fact, Wollstonecraft so much related to Rousseau that she used his phrase 'a genius will educate itself' to describe her first book, written at the same time as she was discovering *Emile*, *Mary: A Fiction* (1989, vol I, 'Prefatory note').

It is probable that she had not finished reading *Emile* when she endorsed it: she had not read the final part, where Rousseau discusses the education of his now-grown tutee's wife-to-be, Sophie. Sophie is taught to obey and please her husband. Because she is a woman, she is deemed incapable of more abstract learning, and dangerous for her lack of morals. A few years later, Wollstonecraft spent a great part of her fifth chapter in the *Vindication*, titled 'Animadversions', explaining how and why Rousseau was wrong. Still, one may ask, why not simply ignore that final chapter of *Emile*, and then reclaim everything Rousseau had written for boys, applying it to girls? After all, *Emile* is a long book, and it's not clear how many readers did make it to the end. And even among those who did, some chose to ignore the final chapter. The Roland couple, for instance, who were political and intellectual actors in the French Revolution and great admirers of Rousseau, chose to devise an educational programme for their daughter Eudora from Rousseau, conveniently forgetting that Eudora was not male (Bergès 2022b, 87).

If one were cynical, one might think that Wollstonecraft, in writing up her own educational programme for boys and girls together, is simply pink-washing Rousseau. Her educational plan, on that account, would be just as useless as the pink razors or pens tagged 'specially designed for women', which customers make fun of in online reviews. Women do not need special pens, especially when the only difference is the colour. But this is a good marketing ploy, and one might have thought that Wollstonecraft or her publisher understood this. Couldn't Wollstonecraft simply have embraced Rousseau's educational model, but apply it to girls as well as boys? There are many reasons why it wouldn't have been a good idea for Wollstonecraft to do this. One is that there is a possibility, a suspicion, that Rousseau himself adapted his educational programme from one written earlier by Gabrielle Suchon, who wrote a treatise on the education of girls which argued that 'rational self-education, personal autonomy and an emphasis on conscience are goods in themselves, for all and not just as they apply to women' (Stanton and Wilkin 2010, liv). Michelle Le Doeuff notes in her *Sex of Knowing* (2003, 45–6) that Rousseau may well have come across Suchon's books in Madame de Warens's library at Les Charmettes. If this is indeed true, then we have a big philosophical scandal on our hands, but also it would be odd to think of Wollstonecraft's educational theory as pink-washing Rousseau if Rousseau's theory was a blue-washing of Suchon.

The biggest worry in reclaiming Rousseau verbatim for girls is that of women's invisibility: if we simply take a programme designed for boys and apply it to girls in a world where boys and girls are not treated equally, then women are going to be ill-served by it. One very early example of this argument comes from Heloise of Argenteuil, the twelfth-century philosopher known for her correspondence and ill-fated marriage with fellow philosopher Abelard (and incidentally the inspiration for Rousseau's own Heloise). As the Abbess of the Benedictine convent of the Paraclete, Heloise felt she needed to rewrite the rule prescribed by Benedict as it was not suitable for women (Levitan 2007, 107). Benedict recommended that monks wear the woollen clothes directly, that is, with no underwear. But this, Heloise pointed out, was not going to work for women who bled once a month. Another – amusing – example she gives is related to wine: she claims, citing Aristotle, that a woman's monthly period acts as a purgation and that this means women safely can, and therefore should be permitted to, consume more alcohol than men with their dinner. Heloise's concerns have an echo in twenty-first-century author Caroline Criado-Perez, who argues with many examples that using 'man' as a universal leads to women being rendered invisible. She cites the testing of car safety belts, which, with the recent exception of Volvo, are only tested on male-sized dummies (Criado-Perez 2019, 186). Again, the well-known list of symptoms for heart attack, it turns out, is a list of symptoms men, but not women, are likely to experience (214).

In philosophy, if we habitually take 'man' to mean 'human', we forget that families exist, that they have their own dynamics, their own work, which often doesn't get represented in the list of men's concerns. Politics is considered to be what happens outside the home, and what happens inside the home is private life. This is true even decades after the slogan 'the personal is the political' forced us to look inside the so-called private sphere. Concepts of independence, for instance, are concepts that can easily be fitted to a man's life, that is, the life of someone who does not have caring duties, and who is catered for at home by a wife. And when women attempt to appropriate this concept of independence, they are forced to employ other women to work in their homes and do the support work needed to keep independence afloat and children thriving (see Young 1995).

None of this amounts to an argument in favour of difference feminism. But we need to remember that what gets defined for men, in a world where men are privileged over women, cannot simply be universalized. If women fail to receive a decent education because they are merely brought up to please and obey men, then men are educated to expect this service from women, and do not learn how to care for themselves or others. So universalizing Rousseau's *Emile*, or at least extending it to middle- and upper-class European girls, will not provide a solution: it will simply mean that no one is taught how to care for a child or how to prepare (or order) a meal. Or, put simply, if mothers in Wollstonecraft's England had simply started to behave like fathers, no one would ever have been at home to care for the children. This is why she insists, throughout the *Vindication of the Rights of Woman*, that the first condition for women to become better mothers is for men to become better fathers. The two must change their ways of living and meet somewhere in the middle.

When we read Wollstonecraft for her views on education, we look for the ways in which girls, in particular, tended to be mis-educated (and still are!). But there is more to Wollstonecraft's view of childhood than the failure to turn little girls into human adults. She also considers what it means to be a child, and what it means to be a parent, and she asks questions that we still haven't answered: what is the relationship between a good parent and their child supposed to be? How do parents protect and educate without dominating? Or is some degree of domination necessary?

CHAPTER 6

Working for a Living

Work features prominently in Wollstonecraft's writings as in her life. She worked from an early age, not because she had to, as women from a lower class would, but because she desperately wanted to escape a family situation that was difficult to live with (her father was a gambler and an alcoholic who physically abused his wife), and she foresaw that if she did not take her life into her own hands, she would probably end up marrying badly or being forced into a type of work she was not suited to. She experimented with being a companion or a private tutor, but decided that they were not a good fit for her as they required more subservience than she was capable of. Running a school and teaching was hard work and not something that could be relied on to earn a living for those doing it – she ended up in debt. In the end, her own skill set and temperament meant that writing for a living was what she could do best. Many of us would think her lucky. But having found something that suited her so well did not stop her noticing that there simply weren't enough options available for women, and that meant they missed out on the chance to live independent lives. This chapter offers an analysis of what this meant for Wollstonecraft.

Education as Training

Wollstonecraft was not the first woman philosopher to claim that women should be educated, but she was perhaps one of the first to claim that this education should lead to something other than marriage or quiet spinsterhood. She saw education both as developing our natural faculties, and as preparation for life's work. But life's work meant more to Wollstonecraft than caring for a husband or child.

The history of philosophy is replete with advice to women to become educated. In the first or second century, a text signed Perictione expounds women's virtues, explaining that a woman who nurtured her wisdom and temperance could rule a city in principle, but that she should best use her virtue to guard over her marital bed, and find a way of putting up with cheating or violent husbands.[1] In the fifteenth century, French philosopher Christine de Pisan argued that women were as capable of benefiting from an education as men, but that they should not use their intelligence to step out of their womanly place in society, because that, she says, is God-assigned: men work outside and women in the home. Women, she concludes, after pages and pages of examples of womanly excellence, could use their moral and intellectual strength to learn to exercise patience, so that if they were married to a violent or dissolute man, they would be able to suffer in silence (Pisan 1982, 117–8, 254–5). At the beginning of the eighteenth century, philosopher Mary Astell made a strong case for why women should be educated to the highest degree, but this was so that they might bear the social isolation of marriage. If Hortense Mancini had been educated, she said of the famous French divorcee who was her neighbour in Chelsea, she would not have felt the need to run away from her violent and deeply unpleasant husband. She would have relied on her inner resources to stay in her marriage (Astell 2015, 94).

Wollstonecraft's arguments that women should be educated because they are just as capable of virtue and intellectual prowess as men are by no means new, then. But what is new is that she regards education as training women for something other than married life. Firstly, as she notes in her earliest work, *Thoughts on the Education of Daughters*, not all women who might expect marriage as their destiny, that is, women from the middle or aristocratic classes, will in fact get married (1989, Vol 1, 69). They might be left without a dowry – essential for a good marriage, as a respectable man will not take a wife who does not bring with her the means of partially supporting herself and her children. A large family may not be able to provide a dowry for all their daughters. Or they may simply not be in a position to arrange social occasions where their daughters might meet potential suitors. Or the daughter may be

---

[1] See Dutsch (2020, 232).

uninterested enough in marriage that she is able to put off suitors. But, Wollstonecraft laments, these women are not educated for anything but marriage. And even if they were, very few positions would be open to them: that of companion, school teacher, or governess, all of which she deems demeaning for an educated woman (having tried all these herself). And the field, she further notes, is diminishing:

> The few trades which are left, are now gradually falling into the hands of the men. (1989, vol 4, 26)

There were certainly trades open for women still when Wollstonecraft wrote, but fewer than there had been just a few decades earlier. Women, according to Amy Louise Erickson (2008), made up a small but significant proportion of trade in London in the first half of the eighteenth century, working mostly in the production of luxury items, as milliners, haberdashers, and shoemakers, but also as clockmakers and even pharmacists. We know from Wollstonecraft's own writings that women could still be jailors and midwives – although the latter may have been one of the occupations taken over by men, following the French fashion of having male doctors, *accoucheurs*, attend a birth (2014, 177). The battle between men and women over the role of assisting births started in eighteenth-century France, when 'educated' men decided that they would be better suited for the job than their female counterparts. Midwives, or *sage-femmes*, did not study medicine at university (as they were not allowed), but learned their trade from other midwives. In France – where men first started to replace women as birth assistants – as well as learning how to assist women in giving birth, the *sage-femmes* were qualified to baptize an infant, even before it was out of its mother, if it looked like it might die. This may well have added the charge of 'superstition' to that of ignorance and helped to push women out of the profession (Adams 1816; Sheridan 2011). One possible reason why accoucheurs became more popular than midwives in England is that they brought with them new life-saving technology, the forceps, which could be used for emergency extractions (Wilson 1995, 187). Godwin himself decided to call on a male physician when Mary Wollstonecraft was in difficulty after giving birth to her second daughter. Unfortunately, medical progress hadn't gotten as far as an understanding of germs, and the doctor's unwashed hands, or his unsterilized equipment, resulted in an infection which killed Wollstonecraft.

One clear way of avoiding midwives being replaced by men would have been to train women to become physicians. But that was not allowed. Some women succeeded nonetheless, including Margaret King, who had been Wollstonecraft's favourite pupil when she was a governess in Ireland. Margaret King, after breaking off an unhappy marriage, trained as a physician at the University of Jena, but to do so she had to dress as a man. Although the battle might have been fought by Wollstonecraft's followers (or at least one follower), it was far from won.

The story of how midwives were replaced by accoucheurs illustrates the point Mary Wollstonecraft is making about women's professions very nicely. Up till then, women's professions and women's education had been considered as entirely separate matters. Philosophers such as Pizan and Astell had argued that women, upper or middle class, ought to be educated to satisfy their intellectual curiosity, and give their minds something to occupy itself with when their married lives proved less than satisfactory. But Wollstonecraft argues that women (also mostly upper class or middle class) should be educated to work, and that their intellect will be better served and more useful if they have a variety of professions to train for, rather than passively falling into one of the few professions which the lady-like education they received makes it possible for them to do – governess, teacher, or companion.

Work and Class

In the second *Vindication*, Wollstonecraft argues that women may usefully study and practise medicine, and pursue political or academic careers, reading politics or history. They could also, she says, be businesswomen, depending on what their natural talents and inclinations were. The main point of having this choice would be to avoid falling into the trap of 'common and legal prostitution' (2014, 177), for if women could earn a living of their own, they 'would not then marry for support', nor, presumably, have to resort to selling sex on the street, as Jemima in the *Wrongs of Women* did.

But the women whose choices Wollstonecraft wishes to broaden are not working-class women. Working-class women did not, on the whole, marry for support, but continued supporting themselves through hard work once they were married. Nor were they educated in such a way that they could fall back on the kind of jobs Wollstonecraft thinks so despicable because they place a woman only slightly above the servant class: teaching, or being a companion. Working-class women, at least some of them, were servants.

Wollstonecraft seems to be aware of the class distinction at play and tries to use it to her advantage. Many women from the poorer classes, she says, 'maintain their children by the sweat of their brows, and keep together families that the vice of the fathers would have scattered abroad' (2014, 104). In doing so, Wollstonecraft says, they act 'heroically', in sharp contrast with gentle women who are 'too indolent to be actively virtuous, and are softened rather than refined by civilization'. The problem with genteel education, she concludes, is that it 'leaves the mind to rust' and, by occupying it with trifles, turns women into 'triflers' (104).

Wollstonecraft does not think, however, that life as a servant, or even a milliner (whom she thinks of as just one step up from prostitutes (2014, 178)), is enviable, and she does think that the condition of working-class women can also be improved through education.

> After the age of nine, girls and boys, intended for domestic employments, or mechanical trades, ought to be removed to other schools, and receive instruction, in some measure appropriated to the destination of each individual, the two sexes being still together in the morning; but in the afternoon, the girls should attend a school, where plain-work, mantuamaking, millinery, &c. would be their employment. (2014, 199)

Does this programme not more or less replicate what was already in place in eighteenth-century Britain? No: for one thing, not every child went to school. There were few schools for girls, and they were of dubious quality, and the poor had to rely on charity schools and not having to work. What Wollstonecraft is proposing is a day school attended by students from all classes, following the model proposed by the Marquis de Talleyrand (to whom she dedicated the *Vindication of the Rights of Woman*) for revolutionary France. Secondly, she suggests that working-class children of 'superior abilities' should be allowed to join those 'of fortune' in a different school, where they might be taught 'the dead and living languages, the elements of science, and continue the study of history and politics, on a more extensive scale, which would not exclude polite literature' (2014, 199).

Wollstonecraft's model does not attempt to break through the class structure – it would be unreasonable to expect a post-Marxist awareness of class struggle in an eighteenth-century author. But she is very aware of the different ways in which women from different classes are oppressed in the societies she knows. And that awareness emerges in her writings. But she does write more about middle- and upper-class women, more about the failings of their education, and the professional choices they ought to have. This is to be at least partly accounted for by her own statement: middle-class women are her audience because they are the ones most likely to change, upper-class women being 'ruined' by their social position and education, and working-class ones being too busy working to stop and think about oppression. Is there more to it than this? Is Wollstonecraft, middle-class herself, incapable of showing a real and lasting interest in working-class women? Something she says in chapter 9 of the *Vindication of the Rights of Woman* suggests a certain elitism that is tied to class:

> Still to avoid misconstruction, though I consider that women in the common walks of life are called to fulfil the duties of wives and mothers, by religion and reason, I cannot help lamenting that women of a superiour cast have not a road open by which they can pursue more extensive plans of usefulness and independence. (2014, 176)

One might want to criticize Wollstonecraft for this attitude to working-class women, in the same way that one might want to criticize Marx for failing to see that women were doubly exploited: by their employers, and by men. It is important to point out that her theory is far from perfect, but her imperfections can be worked on; they are not parts of the system, in the way that some sexism, racism, and classism of past philosophers cannot be separated from the essence of their theory.

Forced to Be Independent

A working woman is independent in the sense that she does not depend on someone else's goodwill for her survival, but depends only on her ability to carry on earning money through her labour. There are obvious problems with this claim: for many, then as now, whether we are able to carry on working is sometimes dependent on the goodwill of another. If a maid in Wollstonecraft's time was found to be pregnant, as Jemima was in *Maria or the Wrongs of Woman*, whether or not her employer will keep her on is entirely dependent on their goodwill. Because Jemima's employer was her rapist, she was not kept on. Nowadays the goodwill which workers depend on is often that of a person they do not know, who decides to sell or buy shares, and restructure the work place, losing some jobs in the process. There is, in Wollstonecraft, a certain idealization of work in general (though she does strongly criticize certain professions in particular) which we find mostly in pre-Marxist thought. W. E. B Dubois, for instance, noted that in his teenage years (the mid-nineteenth century) neither he nor his contemporaries questioned whether workers were exploited, and they believed that one could become rich and flourish simply by being hard-working (Du Bois 2014, 54).

Wollstonecraft seems to move between the claim that independence is to be gained through work, and the claim that only some kinds of work, and sometimes no work at all (provided one is rich), can bring independence. In other words, she moves between independence as a kind of income-generating activity and independence as simply possessing money. But whichever meaning we pick, independence was clearly important to her thought. The very first paragraph of the *Vindication* is a call for independence:

> Independence I have long considered as the grand blessing of life, the basis of every virtue – and independence I will ever secure by contracting my wants, though I were to live on a barren heath. (2014, 21)

For someone in Wollstonecraft's situation, the only way of life open to her – had she not succeeded in earning a living – would have been marriage. And as she could not rely on her father for an introduction (he was a drunk who had remarried a 'disreputable' woman after his wife's death, and therefore did not move in polite society), she would have had to rely on her brother, Edward. But the two did not get along. As a child he had been the favourite, and Mary had suffered from being ignored by her mother. As an adult, he had introduced one of Mary's sisters, Eliza, to her husband. Eliza had married, become pregnant, given birth, and suffered from a breakdown during which she seems to have revealed to Mary that her husband abused her, and begged Mary to rescue her. Mary obliged, and the sisters became runaways, having to hide from Eliza's husband, who had legal rights over her. Under the circumstances, it was unlikely that Edward would have wanted to help Mary find a husband, or that Mary would have agreed to let him pick one for her.

Eliza was not particularly grateful to her sister for the rescue. When she left her husband, she had to leave her baby behind, and the baby died in her father's care. Their other sister, Everina, also felt she had reason to complain: she would not, after her sister's escape, ever be able to marry. Nor could she persuade their brother, who was quite well off compared with the rest of the family, to support her. Mary, then, became unofficial guardian to both her sisters, responsible for their being able to make a living for themselves, or else having to support them financially. The sisters would have preferred the latter: if Mary was so keen on working and making money, why couldn't she make enough for all three of them? But Mary chose instead to have her sisters become teachers in the school she set up in Newington Green. When that didn't work out, and when it was clear that it was their lack of aptitude and enthusiasm that had killed the school, she decided to pay for them to be trained as teachers, and to find posts for them. One sister was sent to Paris to study French. Another was placed in a school in Wales. Both resented the work, the poverty, and the enforced spinsterhood, as well as their separation from one another.

Was it unfair of the Wollstonecraft sisters to blame Mary for their fate, and to expect her to support them as they could no longer be supported by men? Eliza and Everina were not, by any account, particularly pleasant women. Their letters do not show them in a particularly good light. And although we do not know the details of what took place, it is at least possible that Eliza persuaded Mary to help her leave her husband, and that Mary gave her help because she thought her sister's life was in danger. It would also have been harder for Mary to earn enough to keep herself and her two sisters afloat. But presumably, she could have done so if she had been willing to take different kinds of work, and if she had refrained from becoming a mother, which meant she had to support someone else still. In other words, she could have sacrificed her own life and career to support her sisters. Why does any of this matter? Because it may help us understand some of the philosophical underpinning of Wollstonecraft's decision to help her sisters in the way she chose to help them, that is, make them work.

There would be something paradoxical about a philosopher who valued independence above all else, and yet turned relatives into her dependents. If Wollstonecraft were to support her sisters, when she could instead help them become independent, that would contradict her view that independence is objectively valuable, and the theory she derives from it, that women must be emancipated, achieve independence, and become full citizens in the same way men are. At the same time, there seems to be something wrong with telling others that they must be independent and be independent in a certain way. For Eliza and Everina, this meant that the decision how to live their lives was taken from them by their sister. Wollstonecraft, following Rousseau in the *Social Contract*, was forcing her sisters to be free.

Rousseau's pronouncement that those who want to disobey the law established by the general will must be 'forced to be free' is infamous. Forced freedom is no freedom, and it has a definite Orwellian resonance.[2] But Rousseau scholars agree that the statement is a subtle one which does not contradict itself. Rousseau believed that joining the civil state meant leaving the unreflective animal life and becoming a fully moral being. But this belonging to the civil state carried a duty of participation, and a duty not to harm the general will. One who disobeyed the law failed to participate fully in the state that they had created as part of the general will, and inevitably also caused harm. The authoritarian stance towards the offender thus comes from a desire to prevent a particular interest from interfering with the general will. It thus protects the civil state from the individual. But by putting a stop to the action of a particular interest, we are also preventing a reversal of the change from unthinking brute to moral person, as it is moving away from appetite, or private desire, that constitutes the growth of freedom and the transformation of a human being from being a slave to the body to being master of oneself.[3]

---

[2] I agree with Sandra Newman that this term is mostly overused and misused, but it seems appropriate here. www.theguardian.com/books/2023/oct/07/orwellian-nightmares-george-orwell-rage-culture-rewriting-1984
[3] Here I draw from Affeldt (1999, 308–10).

In his *Emile*, Rousseau takes the thought one step further. Because there is no place in the Social Contract for particular wills, dependence on other people ought to be discouraged. Such dependence, he thinks, inevitably places one person or group in a position of subordination: 'Dependence on men, [. . .] engenders all the vices, and by it, master and slave are mutually corrupted.'[4] If Wollstonecraft were to financially support her sisters, then she would corrupt both them and herself by forcing them into a situation of subordination. By helping them find work, she is helping them assert and defend their moral status.

Not that her sisters would have been pleased to be offered a Rousseauian defence of their being obliged to do work they did not enjoy, but they might at least have had the chance to reply:

What if, they might have said, we choose to remain dependent? Rousseau's argument did not apply, after all, to women, and Wollstonecraft herself seemed to believe that not all women could be useful to society by leaving the home. Granted that the life of an unmarried woman dependent on male relatives was very unpleasant indeed, what would have been wrong with Wollstonecraft making a small home for herself and her sisters, and living a quiet domestic life together, with Wollstonecraft earning enough by writing or teaching for the three of them?

Here I want to turn to a more modern take on the issue of women's choice to remain at home, one developed by Anca Gheaus (2008). Gheaus argues that a society that cared about establishing gender parity would think twice about instituting Basic Income, because it would encourage women to stay at home more than they do already. A woman who makes money from staying at home and pleases her partner and relatives by not challenging traditions may feel she is better off than one struggling to make enough money to pay for childcare and at the same time having to answer a constant barrage of questions from people around her about why she bothers. One question is: why can't women choose to be housewives, or full-time mothers? Why do they have to put their career, or education, or any other out-of-home activity before mothering? The argument Gheaus offers is that choosing to be a paid housewife would simply reinforce existing gender prejudices, and make

---

[4] See also James (2013, 19–21) for a discussion of this point.

it less likely that those prejudices could ever be made to disappear or diminish. Eliza and Everina see nothing wrong with living domestic lives, and they see the independence work would bring as a necessity rather than a privilege. Social expectations are both at play and reinforced in the sisters' preferences: that is, they cannot imagine themselves as independent, and by choosing to remain dependent, they show the world that this might be, after all, the best situation for women to be in.

The application of Gheaus's argument to Wollstonecraft's decision not to support her sisters' domesticity has its limits. Wollstonecraft is not a state deciding to facilitate staying at home for a whole nation of women. She is an individual who feels she has to help her sister and is deciding how best she can do that. So there is, perhaps, a stronger and less acceptable element of paternalism in her decision than there is in Gheaus's argument.

Finally, there are limits as to how much philosophy one can derive from a slice of life. Wollstonecraft was trying to do the best she could for herself, her sisters, and later her daughter with an insecure income, and as she died before her sisters did, it is probably just as well that she helped them make a living for themselves rather than depend on her labour. But we should also note that Wollstonecraft was in fact financially supporting others – helping one brother move to the United States, and helping support her friend Fanny's family after the latter's death. Her support was not always unconditional, but she did try to make sure that others besides her could be relieved from poverty sufficiently to have a fighting chance of becoming independent.

Wages for Housework

To be fair to Wollstonecraft's sisters, they were proposing not that Wollstonecraft simply paid them a living, but that they should 'keep house' for her, that is, live with her, keep her company, and see to all domestic matters, while Mary kept writing and teaching to earn a living. In other words, they wanted to be their sister's wives. This leads to a different issue from the one we raised before, different but related. Why can't keeping house count as a job? And why is there something wrong with choosing to be a housewife, over and above the fact that one is thereby dependent on a wage-earning partner? Let's clarify: if someone was paid a wage to keep house for their own family, would this not count as work? And then would this be acceptable to Wollstonecraft as an independent and worthwhile life, in the way that simply being a wife may not be?

Part of the argument against wages for housework would be the argument Gheaus made against Basic Income in gender asymmetrical societies. Paying women to pick up after men, to feed them and make sure they have a comfortable home life, is tantamount to giving them a good reason not to pursue their own career goals. If they live in a society that normalizes women as housewives, then rewarding them financially for doing it will reinforce the idea that this is what they are supposed to do. It will also make it harder to try something else: after all, what guarantee of success is there outside the home? Very little. And if staying at home means getting a regular income, thereby adding to one's current comfort and future security, then the risk of losing this may not seem worth taking. And this is especially true in the eighteenth century, where very few women would risk striking out on their own unless they had to, simply because the framework for career women was mostly non-existent.

Another way of looking at the question is to see the wages not simply as money but as a political statement. This is Silvia Federici's take in her 1975 'Wages against housework':

> But the wage at least recognizes that you are a worker, and you can bargain and struggle around and against the terms and the quantity of that wage, the terms and the quantity of the work. To have a wage means to be part of a social contract, and there is no doubt concerning its meaning: you work, not because you like it, or because it comes naturally to you, but because it is the only condition under which you are allowed to live. Exploited as you might be, you are not that work. (Federici 1975, 76)

Women in gender asymmetrical societies or patriarchal societies who perform domestic work without being paid for it are accepting that this is their natural role, that which they are born to do, and that which will make them, and everyone else, happiest. So, Federici argues, wanting to be paid for it is an expression of a refusal that this work is 'the expression of our nature'. On the contrary, if we refuse to be paid for the work we do in the home, we are accepting a status quo in which women are submissive dependents: 'It is also clear that if we think we do not need that money, it is because we have accepted the particular forms of prostitution of body and mind by which we get the money to hide that need.' Here Federici echoes Wollstonecraft, who wrote that women, if they were educated, might pursue business of various kinds, 'which might save many from common and legal prostitution' (177). But Federici anticipates that women may not be educated and still deserve to escape the prostitution of an unequal marriage. Is this something that Wollstonecraft could not even contemplate, as it would have required a social framework that was non-existent, that is, for the government to pay out wages to women, or enforce the payment by husbands and relatives? Both these options were unthinkable. The only relief the government provided for anyone not being able to meet their own needs was the poor-house, which was really a sort of prison. And far from being in a position to demand that husbands pay their wives a wage, English law in the eighteenth century (and until the end of the nineteenth) defined married women as 'covered', which meant that any income a woman received from her work in principle belonged to her husband. In practice, this meant that women could not strike out on their own and achieve independence if they were already married. This extended to other countries. After Hortense Mancini, the French divorcee whom Mary Astell discusses in her *Reflections on Marriage*, ran away from her husband, she tried to achieve independence through an income paid her by the King of France, but the law was such that her (already very rich) husband had no difficulty seizing that income. Mancini then escaped to England, where at least it became more difficult for her husband to reach into her pockets. In the nineteenth century, a British woman, Caroline Norton, also left her husband when he became so violent that it constituted a threat to her life. She attempted to make a living by writing, but her husband was consistently able to claim her earnings as his.[5]

That a scheme such as wages for housework was unthinkable does not entail that Wollstonecraft did not think it. And she comes very close to saying so in *A View of the French Revolution*, when she says: 'Nature, having made men unequal, by giving stronger bodily and mental powers

---

[5] For Hortense Mancini, see Astell (2015), and for Caroline Norton, see Frazer (2021).

to one than to another, the end of government ought to be to destroy this inequality by protecting the weak' (1989, vol 6, 17). While Wollstonecraft does not believe that women have inferior mental powers to men, and while her statements on women's supposed bodily inferiority do not, we saw, represent her views in a straightforward manner, she does seem to believe that the mothering of infants falls by nature to women. And mothering infants, instead of working to support oneself, is very much weakening in its effect. A woman who gives her time and energy to ensuring the health, safety, and well-being of a child, trusting the child's father to make sure that she herself does not starve, is in a vulnerable position. It's not a huge leap, then, to read what Wollstonecraft says in *A View of the French Revolution* as recommending that the state ensures the material independence of women who are in charge of infants and children.

Ultimately Mothers

Despite her calls for equality, for women to become independent citizens who are responsible for their own upkeep rather than dependent on husbands, Wollstonecraft still thinks that most women should become wives and mothers and stay home and look after children: 'women in the common walks of life are called to fulfil the duties of wives and mothers, by religion and reason' (2014, 176). Motherhood, we saw in a previous chapter, is a 'grand duty' and one which, if it is not properly fulfilled, will lead to the stripping of the title of citizen. This means that, for Wollstonecraft, performing the duties of motherhood is working for the state. But only in that very restricted sense, as Wollstonecraft expects, at least for middle-class women, that it will be the husband, not the state, who will reward the work of motherhood materially and financially.

> I have then viewed with pleasure a woman nursing her children, and discharging the duties of her station with, perhaps, merely a servant maid to take off her hands the servile part of the household business. I have seen her prepare herself and children, with only the luxury of cleanliness, to receive her husband, who returning weary home in the evening found smiling babes and a clean hearth. My heart has loitered in the midst of the group, and has even throbbed with sympathetic emotion, when the

scraping of the well-known foot has raised a pleasing tumult. Whilst my benevolence has been gratified by contemplating this artless picture, I have thought that a couple of this description, equally necessary and independent of each other, because each fulfilled the respective duties of their station, possessed all that life could give. (2014, 172)

Here the dependence is mutual and recognized as such so that it does not require that women be 'subordinated'. Does this mean they do not depend on their husband for a living? No, but Wollstonecraft is not? talking of the couple as being poor or wealthy; they are a financial unit who, presumably because of their interdependence, choose together how to spend their money (2014, 173).

The key to a solution here lies in Wollstonecraft's conception of the ideal marriage, where wife and husband are friends before they are lovers, and let their reason lead them in choosing each other as partners, rather than their emotions, physical desire, or ambition. Nancy Kendrick has explained this conception of marriage in terms of Aristotelian friendship. Aristotle distinguished between two kinds of friendships: virtue friendship and utility friendship. Utility friendship typically involves some sort of complementarity of roles and requires inequalities of wealth, knowledge, age, or, only in the case of marriage, gender (NE1159b13-15, 1158b12-14). Virtue friendships, on the other hand, rely on equality and each partner caring for the other's moral character and development.

By appealing to friendship and virtue, according to Kendrick, Wollstonecraft attempts to move marriage 'from the realm of the transactional and place it in the realm of the moral' (40). In other words, marriage is not about swapping services – whether domestic, sexual, or financial – but about helping each other become 'a fully articulated moral agent, one who gives and receives goodwill for who she is' (49). In such a marriage, a woman who spends some years financially dependent on her husband because she is raising their children is less likely to be subordinated, and she can be confident that her husband regards any other goals she might have as merely on hold, and that he will fulfil his own duties as a father and enable her own ambitions once nature no longer requires her to be the main carer.

Unfortunately, this view of marriage is very much an ideal in Wollstonecraft's scheme, one that it will take time to realize. In order to be worthy of the sort of friendship that such a marriage requires, and capable of offering it, one must have good judgement and virtuous character. However, society is such, Wollstonecraft tells us, that women – depending on their class – are either drudges or triflers, and men not much better. Can housework and childcare ever be more than transactional work at worst, and a huge leap of faith at best? A woman who marries a husband chosen for her – and who has not been educated to make the best of her situation or seek the friendship of her husband – will inevitably find herself in a situation of legal prostitution. But what about a woman who values reason and virtue, who marries a man who also does, and whose marriage is based on the sort of friendship Kendrick describes? Even then, marrying represents a high risk. A woman, in eighteenth-century society, gives up all her rights to her husband when she enters into the marriage contract. It follows that she has to trust that the friendship they have will hold throughout their common lives. This perhaps explains Wollstonecraft's initial reluctance to marry Godwin.

The early days of the Wollstonecraft–Godwin marriage (and early days is all they had) seem to reflect the sort of Aristotelian friendship Kendrick had in mind. But their union was unusual in that both worked as writers for a living, and there was no question that Wollstonecraft would give up her own work to care for their daughters. The couple lived apart – but across from each other – and Fanny lived with her mother, but spent time at Godwin's. Their living arrangements also meant less domestic work: no family dinners to organize every evening, no parties, and no keeping out of Godwin's way when he wanted to write. So while their couple was not entirely gender-symmetrical, it was perhaps as symmetrical as could be expected for the time, and possibly more gender-symmetrical than many couples nowadays are.

In a sense, a single woman who has an income – as was the case, more or less, for Wollstonecraft herself when she had her first child – is better off than a married one. She is not financially dependent on anyone but herself, so provided she can afford some help and work flexible hours (as Wollstonecraft did) she is free to offer her labour to her child. If she does this freely, she is acting as nature intended (as Wollstonecraft believed), but without a task-master of a husband holding the purse strings and imposing routines or duties which she may not think are best. But, as

Wollstonecraft knew, with single parenting comes much instability, poverty, and hard work. And in many cases, it simply can't be done.

Reading Wollstonecraft on work and independence raises many questions that we yet have to answer. Are marriage and motherhood incompatible with independence because they prevent women from working outside the home and getting to know the world? Or is the main obstacle to independence financial so that if women were to be paid for their housework they would not suffer as they do? Can marriage and parenthood be reformed so as to enable both parties to live independent and fulfilling lives? Or is this still a pipedream?

CHAPTER 7

Philosophy, Progress, and Real Politics

Wollstonecraft's philosophy is shaped by ideals: ideals of virtue, reason, and equality. These are drawn from religion, but also from a deep conviction that human beings are led by reason. She makes it clear, throughout her work, that these ideals are derived from her belief in a god that created human beings to be equal and perfectible, and that furthermore we were created in that god's image in the sense that we are rational creatures. It follows that human lives should always be directed towards moral improvement, and that moral improvement can only happen through the development of reason. So any social or political reform, according to Wollstonecraft, must place an emphasis on the sort of education that will eventually lead to the virtuous development of all. Any structures that put obstacles in the way of this development must be replaced. This includes any inequality-reinforcing structure (whether class-, gender-, or race-based) and any that stunts the growth of reason through domination, such as absolute monarchy.

Wollstonecraft's views on political reforms were in line with the republican thinkers of her time, but are they at all possible to hold on to in the twenty-first century, or are they too infused with the sort of ideology we are wary of? Citizens of democratic states do not, on the whole, wish to be ruled by moralizing leaders, or laws derived from religious books – at least not overtly. They worry that moral ideals will hold us back – prevent us from acknowledging issues and problems that do not appear to fit within a particular ethical scheme. And while admirable, Wollstonecraft's scheme, like any other, is far from flawless.

One way of phrasing this worry is to ask how far is Wollstonecraft from what we would now call political realism? Political realism is a school of thought that regards ideal theory as unsuited to human progress, either because it does not take into account 'real' facts about how human beings behave when they live together or because it does not propose reforms that would actually work.

The key mistakes realists attribute to political philosophers is to think that politics is somehow applied ethics. We first need to identify what the leading moral principles of politics ought to be (e.g. justice), and organize political thought and then actions around them. Philosophers who have recently defended political realism, such as Bernard Williams and Raymond Geuss, have argued that this is getting the logic of politics wrong. The way to evaluate political action is not to look at how closely it matches moral ideals but to look for internal consistency: how do these actions promote the value that is central to politics? That value is, following Hobbes's story of the state, order. Politics is not about ensuring that justice presides in all institutions and laws that regulate human interaction: it is about 'securing order, protection, safety, trust and the conditions of cooperation' (Williams 2005, 3). This means that political thought must pay more attention to history than to moral ideals: 'with special attention to the varieties of ways in which people can structure and organize their actions so as to limit and control forms of disorder that they might find excessive or intolerable for other reasons' (Geuss 2009, 22).

While hard-core political realism would refuse any place for morality in politics, there are more subtle proposals available as to how we might avoid burdening humanity with unrealistic moral or theological goals and duties.[1] But even Bernard Williams seem to have left an opening for virtues, at least, being part of political practice: even if political action must be determined according to its potential to promote the kind of order that is desirable at that time, the politician who acts must be in possession of the kind of character that will enable them to understand that a politically justified action is nonetheless undesirable. Mark Philp, who discusses this, offers Abraham Lincoln as an example: Lincoln claimed to be doing his best, but was aware that his actions would, in the end, be judged not by their moral worth but according to whether the 'judgments and commitments' behind his decisions turned out to be correct (Philp 2012, 639). There is a place for character, then, in political

---

[1] See for instance Sagar and Sabl, 2018.

realism, and where there is a place for character, there is a place for virtue. So a republican-styled political realism would look quite different, perhaps, from a more liberal one.

One such proposal comes from Philip Pettit (2017), who explains political realism in terms of what political thinkers should avoid in order to keep moralizing out of politics without eliminating the idea that some form of morality, that is, virtue, can remain part of politics. His proposal takes the form of the following clauses:

(1) Anti-moralism. Political philosophy should begin from the concerns of people in the society for which it prescribes, not from an imported set of ethical principles.
(2a) Anti-deontologism. In extracting a normative ideal from those concerns, it should identify a collective target for the citizenry to track, not a collective constraint that they should satisfy.
(2b) Anti-transcendentalism. The ideal or set of ideals it adopts should be capable of guiding people's judgements of their actual society and their actions within it.
(3) Anti-utopianism. In putting forward those ideals for the guidance of members, it should focus on feasible initiatives and sustainable institutions, not just on ideal measures.
(4) Anti-vanguardism. And in putting forward those ideals, it should not pronounce on what is right and wrong without acknowledging the claims of democracy (Pettit 2017, 332–3).

Focusing on 1–3 (leaving 4 aside, as democracy was not yet established, so it is not reasonable to hold this as an expectation), I want to show that Wollstonecraft's proposal was in fact compatible with this form of political realism. Firstly, while anything Wollstonecraft prescribes is unlikely to be stripped of either morality or religion, she does take her cue from reflections on human nature, and in particular a state of nature theory, in order to devise her political philosophy. In the first section, we will see how that works, and how she derives the conclusion that in order to live together successfully we must develop certain virtues. This will also address (2a): what her idea of success is tracking is always human happiness and the common good, rather than any requirement about how we should behave. Next – and this addresses (2b) – while she believes human beings should be religious, she also has strong sympathies with what Rousseau would call civic religion, that is, a set of beliefs adapted to the needs of the commonwealth, and tracking the common good. This will be the topic of the second section. Finally, her views on political economy, and in particular her endorsement of Turgot's views, are an excellent example of (3) how she privileges feasibility over ideals, or at least insists that we should question ideals that are not suited to practices that are conducive to human happiness. I will discuss this in the third section.

What Are We Like? State of Nature and Human Progress: Anti-moralism and Anti-deontologicalism

Progress and self-knowledge go hand in hand. As Rousseau said in the Preface of his *Second Discourse*: 'For how can the source of inequality among men be known unless one begins by knowing men themselves?' (Rousseau 2018, 122). And at the same time, he adds, in order to be philosophers enough to reflect on this, we need to have progressed so much that we have departed from our primitive state to the point that we can no longer recognize it. This makes Rousseau's project of retracing the progress of humanity to understand, for instance, how injustice came to be part of human life complicated, to say the least. Rousseau lacked the evidence for the story of human political progression which he proposed, and recent anthropological and archeological research has cast serious doubt on it, suggesting that there are in fact not one but many stories to be told.[2] But we can also use the relationship between progress and self-knowledge in a forward-looking strategy, that is, understand ourselves better so we know which reforms might work best and which are more likely to fail. For example, if you want to get better at playing the piano (or the ukulele), you don't just need to practise. You need to assess what stage you are at, what your relevant abilities and existing training are, the time you have available, your willingness to spend that time practising, and your ambitions regarding the instrument. Are you the kind of person who can make time every day for a short practice? Will you get bored and give up in a few months (if so, better to invest in a ukulele than a grand piano)? Do you

---

[2] See Graeber and Wengrow, (2021).

know musical theory? Can you read music? Do you like to sing along? Do you want to play in a band, an orchestra, or just strum along to a few songs? Once you have answered these questions, you can plan for progress towards a goal, and build certain expectations – 'next December, I'll be able to play "Last Christmas" on my ukulele. I'll need to practise three times a week for about 15 minutes each time.'

Wollstonecraft, who was mostly self-taught and very knowledgeable in a large number of areas (including Shakespeare's writings and Handel's music), would have known exactly how progress works and how it can be measured, and she applied these insights to the future progress of humanity in general. In the *Vindication of the Rights of Woman*, the second paragraph of the dedication to the Marquis de Talleyrand, she writes that she wishes 'to see woman placed in a station in which she would advance, instead of retarding, the progress of those glorious principles that give a substance to morality' (Wollstonecraft 2014, 21). There are another thirty or so references to progress in the *Vindication*. In the 230 pages of the *Historical and Moral View of the Origin and Progress of the French Revolution*, where she offers her own state-of-nature theory, there are, perhaps unsurprisingly considering the title, forty-six references to the progress of knowledge, reason, truth, principles, or simply society.

Wollstonecraft's motive for speculating on the state of nature in *View of the French Revolution* is forward-looking in that the point of finding out what primitive humanity was like is to gauge its capacity for future progress. The success of the revolution, she says, depends on whether the French are able to behave justly, and that depends on how much their ancestral nature is tamed. Not very, it turns out: 'The stubborn habits of men, whom personal interest kept firm to their ground, it was morally certain would interrupt the tranquil march of the revolution' (1989, vol 6, 145). The stubborn habits, here, are a natural inclination to prefer war to work. War, she argues, is a natural occupation for 'savage man' because it is not, unlike work, 'a kind of abridgment of their liberty' (146). Given the choice between violent chaos and a 9-to-5 existence, she thinks that humans unaccustomed to living with rules naturally prefer the former. The state of nature was, she says, a state of war fed by 'restless temper, and savage manners' and 'passion for war and plunder' more than by necessity (147).

What brought men out of the state of nature, she speculates, were 'social feelings' (1989, vol 6, 146) which were bound to develop in old age, as retired warriors relive their former glory by telling stories to their progeny. By then a person has seen enough suffering that they have developed sympathy, and

> he begins to contemplate, as desirable, associations of men, to prevent the inconveniencies arising from loneliness and solitude.[3] Hence little communities living together in the bonds of friendship, securing to them the accumulated powers of man, mark the origin of society: and tribes, growing into nations, spreading themselves over the globe, form different languages, which producing different interests, and misunderstandings, excite distrust. (146)

In Wollstonecraft's story, as soon as we manage to get out of the state of nature and form societies, we begin the process of dividing up the world into nations that go to war against one another. Is that just because our warring nature must persist? It seems not: becoming domestic, being attached to home is enough, according to her, for a state-of-nature warrior to want to put down arms and become peaceful. So what brings the warrior back? The 'reign of ignorance', Wollstonecraft says, and the manipulation of rulers: 'whilst fools continually argue, from the practice of inhuman savages, that wars are necessary evils, courts have found them convenient to perpetuate their power' (1989, vol 6, 147).

If it is ignorance that forces us back to state-of-nature practices, then what is the solution? True to herself, Wollstonecraft preaches education. The state of nature distinguishes men according to natural genius, she says. The civil state, with its system of hereditary distinctions, negates this by 'cruelly abridging rational liberty'. These distinctions 'have prevented man from rising to his just point of elevation, by the exercise of his improveable faculties' (1989, vol 6, 220). But just as the genius of a few may be squashed by a bad civil state, the intelligence of all can be raised by a good one. Civilization enables the refinement of taste and intellect in those who are already prone to superiority of judgement, she says, but more than that, it makes it possible to improve the judgement

---

[3] This seems to be a response to Rousseau's claim in the *Second Discourse* that the reason savage men do not develop morality is because real sympathy, as opposed to mere animal feeling, requires frequent exposure to the pain of others (2018, 154).

of those who are not. Every one, she says, is 'equally susceptible of common improvement', and a state that does not encourage this 'can be considered in no other light than as a monstruous tyranny, a barbarous oppression, equally injurious to the two parties, though in different ways. For all the advantages of civilization cannot be felt, unless it pervades the whole mass, humanizing every description of men – and then it is the first of blessings, the true perfection of man' (220).

This argument echoes the one she had made three years previously to Talleyrand, in the Dedication to the *Vindication of the Rights of Woman*, claiming of women that 'if she be not prepared by education to become the companion of man, she will stop the progress of knowledge and virtue' (2014, 22). Reason and knowledge, she argued, only work if they are shared. Some skills and knowledge can be partially distributed through a community without harm – indeed, we don't all need to know how to perform an appendectomy, or fly a helicopter – but not so with general reasoning skills, or basic knowledge that is required for daily survival. Imagine yourself in an emergency situation: you are in a room with a large group of people, and the zombies are trying to break in. The door will give way soon. Some of you have been trained and know what to do. There is a secret passage, and you can open it through a voice recognition mechanism. But you need everyone else to be quiet, which means that you need to tell them that survival depends on the mechanism registering your voice. But you can't tell them that if they are screaming in panic. Imagine that you next succeed in quieting everyone for long enough to speak into the microphone. The door opens from the outside. But everyone is rushing towards it and it won't open. Or the passage is narrow, and for everyone to get through you'll need to persuade them to line up. So: you're zombie chow. But had everyone in the room been privy to the escape mechanism, or had they been sensible people who are used to listening to reason in situations of emergencies, you might have been saved.

What goes for emergency situations goes for everyday ones – as any schoolteacher will know, a classroom where only a few students are capable of sitting quietly and taking part in learning activities is not easier to teach than one in which none are. Possibly worse, as one feels bad for the students who are ready to learn.

State of Nature and Human Progress 121

Following this line of argument, Wollstonecraft says that a civil state will fail to grow if it does not educate all its members. France, before the revolution, only grew from the top, educating the rich in some ways – courtly behaviour and some knowledge of the fine arts – but not others, and in particular not in the ways of political liberty. Despite this absence of real progress, Wollstonecraft believed that in the early days of the revolution a sufficient number of people had just enough knowledge and insight to save the day. These people set up

> a simple code of instruction, containing all the truths necessary to give a comprehensive perception of political science; which will enable the ignorant to climb the mount of knowledge, when they may view the ruins of the ingenious fabric of despotism, that has so long disgraced the dignity of man by its odious and debasing claims. (1989, vol 6, 221)[4]

What is interesting about Wollstonecraft's reference to the French revolutionary project of educational reform is her focus on political science.[5] Most efforts at educating a people will level their ambitions at basic numeracy and literacy skills, especially when it comes to primary education. But Wollstonecraft included politics in her educational programmes from the first. In chapter XII of the *Vindication of the Rights of Woman*, where she devises a curriculum for boys and girls, topics are divided into groups according to teaching methods. 'Botany, mechanics and astronomy' are to be taught outdoors, 'reading, writing, arithmetic, natural history, and some simple experiments in natural philosophy' in classrooms, but never for more than one hour at a time without exercise breaks. And the last group, 'the elements of religion, history, the history of man, and politics', are to be taught following the Socratic model of conversation (2014, 199). All this is to take place in primary schools, before children reach the age of nine, at which point

---

[4] The simple code referred to here is either the one drafted by Talleyrand in 1791 or the one by his successor, Condorcet. Condorcet had invited Wollstonecraft to contribute to his report – his published draft states that the project for women's education will be prepared separately, and this is almost certainly what Wollstonecraft was asked to work on. Unfortunately, the Girondins, a group of Republican revolutionaries Condorcet was part of, fell victim to the Terror, and Condorcet's project was never completed. We have good reason to believe that when it was taken up again, culminating in the Loi Daunou on public education, Wollstonecraft's thoughts were taken into consideration (Bergès, 2024).
[5] On this, see Tomaselli (2020, 130).

they are to be divided, by class, means, and ability, into two groups: those who train for employment and those who continue their formal education. The latter will be taught 'the elements of science, and continue the study of history and politics, on a more extensive scale, which would not exclude polite literature' (199).

Wollstonecraft's emphasis on political science is unusual if we compare it to educational programmes that exist nowadays, but we must bear in mind the revolutionary, and republican, context of her work. She is writing about educating children born under a monarchy – where they would have had little or no input into their own government – but hoping to live under a republic. They are not, she says, prepared for republican liberty. And while in the second *Vindication* she is concerned with the education of British children – preparing them for what she hopes will be a more republican future – in *View* she is especially worried that the French may stop the progress of their own revolution, because of their lack of education:

> The character of the French, indeed, has been so depraved by the inveterate despotism of ages, that even amidst the heroism which distinguished the taking of the Bastille, we are forced to see that suspicious temper, and that vain ambition of dazzling, which have generated all the succeeding follies and crime. For, even in the most spirited public-spirited actions, celebrity seems to have been the spur, and the glory, rather than the happiness of frenchmen, the end. This observation inforces the grand truth on mankind, that without morality there can be no great strength of understanding, or real dignity of conduct. (1989, vol 6, 123)[6]

In other words, learning to think about politics is also learning to think about the values that sustain a regime, and in the case of a republic, it is virtue that carries the weight of the system, but in the case of absolute monarchy such as the one France had before 1789, it is, on the contrary, 'vain ambition' and depravation of character – an uneducated subject who has no moral principles to hold on to is much more malleable than a virtuous one concerned with public happiness.

---

[6] Note that this is one of many passages in *View* where Wollstonecraft happily trashes the character of French people. Her remarks are also at times sexist: she criticizes the French for being 'a nation of women' (1989, vol 6, 121).

Wollstonecraft's account of human progress is entirely in tune with the republican and revolutionary thinkers of her time, especially with regard to their emphasis on the need for citizens to be virtuous in order to support their freedom, but it is not an example of purely ideological thinking. Rather than attempting to impose an artificial morality on human beings, one which might interfere with the effectiveness of political actions, she identifies what comes naturally to us – sympathy – and argues that a bad civil state will corrupt this natural trait, while preventing us from developing our reason and knowledge. A good state, that is, a republic, will need to redress this through a strong educational programme, thereby enabling citizens to maintain themselves in the best possible civil state. Their collective target is human happiness, and to achieve this, human beings need to be true to their uncorrupted nature.

God and Politics, or How Not to Lose Your Religion in Paris: Anti-transcendentalism

When Mary Wollstonecraft travelled to Paris, she was intending to write a series of letters to her publisher, Joseph Johnson.[7] This turned into the larger project of a multi-volume book: *An Historical and Moral View of the Origin and Progress of the French Revolution; and the Effect It Has Produced in Europe* (the first and only volume was published in 1794). But she did write to Johnson, and in her first letter she said: 'I am not become an Atheist, I assure you, by residing in Paris' (1989, vol 6, 445). Paris at that time was fermenting with atheism: the friends Wollstonecraft made among the Girondins, the people she got to admire and like, such as Madame Roland, the Marquis de Condorcet, and Jacques-Pierre Brissot, were mostly atheists. But she herself, like her compatriot Thomas Paine, was not an atheist. And unlike Paine, who developed a form of theism inspired by Quakerism, Wollstonecraft's religion was much closer to regular Church of England. This prompts us to ask: how did she reconcile her religion with her more radical political stance? More generally: must one be an atheist to be a radical and to

---

[7] Parts of this section are adapted from the third section of Bergès (2019).

work towards the human progress she was interested in, that is, one that needed its ideals embedded in the real world?

The answer is quite straightforwardly no: Wollstonecraft does not appear to have felt there was a conflict between her religion and happiness-tracking, social-reform-led, human progress. Her philosophy of religion seems to have been subject to Rousseau's influence in two ways. Firstly, private religion, that is, one's relationship with the divine, has to be kept mostly separate from the public sphere. Secondly, she was sympathetic to a version of what Rousseau called civic religion, that is, the organization of institutions such that they fostered reason and the civic virtues deemed necessary for social progress. But because these virtues were measured according to what the society in question needed, this form of civic religion would not be deemed transcendental. Private religion would, but that is not related to politics in Wollstonecraft's case.

Part of the reason why Wollstonecraft did not feel the appeal of atheism as her French friends did was because of her strong rejection of their variety of Christianity, Catholicism, and the way it manifested itself in pre-Revolutionary France. France, according to Wollstonecraft, was over-full with clergymen, most of whom could not be relied on to teach or protect morality: 'France maintained two hundred thousand priests, united in the same spirit of licentiousness' (1989, vol 6, 51). Getting rid of these and their corrupt practices (though hopefully not as they were in fact gotten rid of, murdered on their way to prison in September 1792) was therefore a priority.

Wollstonecraft shared her mistrust of some forms of organized religion with Condorcet. In his final work, *Sketch of the Progress of the Human Mind*, Condorcet had argued that the 'spirit of genius' which drives humanity through various epochs towards progress was driven away by 'tyranny and superstition' with the advent of Judeo-Christian and Muslim religions (Condorcet 2012, 89). Priests both controlled education, and in particular moral education, and at the same time developed a corrupt system whereby crimes could be 'forgiven' in exchange for a payment (2012, 32). The moral system they developed, Condorcet adds, was more superstition than natural morality, and it attempted to regulate natural human behaviour through the imposition of unnatural limitations. Eventually, he argues, through the help of the printing press, which helped disseminate knowledge, dishonest priests would be found out and atheism would naturally spread:

> The intolerance of the priests, their struggle for political power, their scandalous greed and moral depravity made even more disgusting by a mask of hypocrisy, revolted anyone whose soul was uncorrupted, whose mind unclouded, whose heart undaunted. There was such a striking contrast between the dogmas, principles and behaviour of the priests and those of the early disciples, the founders of their doctrine and moral creed, of whom the priests could scarcely keep the people in total ignorance. (Condorcet 2012, 63)

Wollstonecraft agreed with the philosophers of the Enlightenment that religion had for too long been the instrument of suppressing reason and enforcing superstition, thus 'enslaving' the people to the priests, and preventing them from ever freeing themselves. Reason, she argues, must be fully developed in order to want freedom. A system of education which does not encourage independent thought and does not strengthen the intellect results in a stunted mind, which only wants what it has and sees no better future for itself. So just as the peasants of France did not spontaneously rebel as soon as they could, but carried on acting as slaves, rich women do not for the most part have the desire to 'break their chains', but instead value the fact that men fuss over them and give them clothes and jewels for which they 'neither toil nor spin' more than they value reason, freedom, and independence (2014, 83). Any sort of republican government, therefore, must foster the sort of intellectual and moral independence that will enable citizens to recognize and fight domination. And because religion is that which most often robs people of their independence, it must either be reformed accordingly or not made to play a major role in civic life.

While her religious convictions certainly inform her philosophy, Wollstonecraft does not appear to believe that the state should rule through religion. At most, the state's religious intervention should be to prevent superstition from taking over reason, and protect education from the 'priests' who would use it to shape obedient subjects rather than clear-thinking citizens. In that sense her political outlook is clearly anti-transcendentalist, focusing on the civic virtues that are needed to help society develop without domination, and not the imposition of external theistic standards which would obstruct such development and preserve structures of domination.

Bread, Money, and Women: Anti-utopianism

> I hate commerce. [...] You will tell me, that exertions are necessary: I am weary of them!
>
> (1989, vol. 6, 376)

Wollstonecraft's letters to her American lover Imlay are full of comments of this kind. Imlay's business kept him away from her while she was pregnant, and later caring for their child, Fanny. It is natural that Wollstonecraft would have come to resent it. But did it go further than this, and did Wollstonecraft line up with the anti-commercial thinkers, who took their cue from Fenelon's *Telemaque*, and believed that commerce was only detrimental to human happiness? Some of her remarks to Imlay suggest as much: 'Be not too anxious to get money! – for nothing worth having is to be purchased.' And

> [h]ow I hate this crooked business! This intercourse with the world, which obliges one to see the worst side of human nature! Why cannot you be content with the object you had first in view, when you entered into this wearisome labyrinth? -I know very well that you have imperceptibly been drawn on; yet why does one project, successful or abortive, only give place to two others? Is it not sufficient to avoid poverty? (1989, vol 6, 395)

But many of her comments simply address the fact that Imlay was too engrossed by his business to spend time with her and their daughter, and that his business travels overseas were often dangerous, causing her to worry. Was she simply jealous of his work? Or did she feel that it was inappropriate to love such work, or to love it to such an extent as to forget one's family duties? Perhaps both. She didn't like Imlay's 'money-getting face' (1989, vol 6, 373), and nor did she approve of his money-making schemes, which involved exchanging silver sold by desperate aristocrats for food. Imlay – who later cheated on Wollstonecraft – was not, it seems, a particularly admirable man, and may have been involved in the slave trade before coming to Paris (Verhoeven 2006).

Wollstonecraft's ambivalence about commerce did not stem entirely from her private life. In *View*, she sees commerce as a speculative activity, and one that was morally repugnant, especially during times of war: 'What is speculation, she asks, but a species of gambling, I might have said fraud, in which address generally gains the prize?' (1989, vol 6, 304). However, her condemnation of her lover's commercial character or wartime speculation does not amount to a rejection of commercial society in general.[8]

In a 1699 book that was popular at the time when Wollstonecraft wrote, *The Adventures of Telemachus*, Fénelon argued that commerce and luxury were the cause of corruption, and that France, in particular, had better focus on returning to its rural roots than engage in excessive efforts to develop its commercial ties. Rousseau, a follower of Fénelon, developed an account of rural republicanism, arguing in his *Constitutional Project for Corsica* for a strong link between rural life and a citizenry that is both more patriotic (because of being physically attached to the earth) and healthier (because they stay away from towns' pollution and vice). But also, rural life, he argues, is more conducive to freedom, because those who produce the food they need to eat are more likely to be independent from external or arbitrary powers (Rousseau 1765, 10).[9] It is easy to think how a concatenation of Fénelon and Rousseau could end up as a form of utopianism: a world shut off from the sort of technological and cultural effervescence that one finds in cities, and where instead each person lives peacefully in their own home, tilling the earth and eating what they grow. The proponents of commercialism, on the other hand, seem to align with the realists: leave morality aside, let the market shape the activities of the land, and hope for the best.

Commerce was a particularly relevant part of the background of the French Revolution. The French had been impressed by Smith's *The Wealth of Nations*, and they had their own school of economists attempting to work reforms on the old monarchical economical

---

[8] See Carroll 2019 for a great discussion of Wollstonecraft's philosophy of commerce, and Packham 2024 for a study of how all of Wollstonecraft's works were embedded in the emerging field of political economy.
[9] For an excellent introduction to these issues, see Hont (2006). For a discussion of Rousseau's rural republicanism, see Bergès (2016, 112).

frameworks which had led to a profound national debt. Anne-Robert Turgot, Controller General of Finances, who is sometimes described as a physiocrat (and whom Wollstonecraft calls an 'economist'), was critical of the state's stranglehold on the production of grain. While his theories were probably sound, they had very unfortunate historical consequences. Turgot tried to free the price of grain just before a particularly bad harvest in the fall of 1775, and the resulting chaos brought about a severe bout of famine and the so-called flour wars, with riots all over France. Turgot's friend and colleague Condorcet tried to defend him by arguing that freeing the price of wheat was still a good idea as it removed the arbitrary controls that made producers unable to bounce back from a bad harvest. Condorcet also tied the stifling governmental laws and the corruption of the officials implementing them to growing inequalities in the distribution of wealth.

Condorcet later reflected that Turgot's *Reflexions sur la Formation des Richesses* (1766) had planted the seed for the *Wealth of Nations*, published in 1776, while another, less generous commentator wrote that everything that was true in *Wealth of Nations* was also in Turgot's *Reflexions*, and that anything Smith added was wrong (Dupont de Nemours, 1782, *Vie de Turgot*). Condorcet started working with Turgot (as inspector general of the Paris Mint) in 1774, ten years after Smith's visit to Paris, and did not meet Smith. But the two may have corresponded later, and Condorcet sent him a copy of his *Life of Turgot*.

Turgot was forced to resign in 1776 as a result of the riots. But Condorcet stayed in place at the Mint, and pursued a politics of the (relatively) free market. In 1776, he published *Le commerce des blés*, arguing that state interference in the selling and buying of grain, such as was practised in Old Regime France, was harmful not only to the economy but also to the social and moral well-being of the French people. In that book, Condorcet made a strong case for the view that the economic is instrumental to the social and political. He concludes in part 2 of his book: 'Thus, the liberty of grain commerce, by securing more sustenance for the people, and in a manner more equal and better suited to its faculties, will make the people greater, stronger, less degraded and less corrupt.'[10]

---

[10] The following two paragraphs are adapted from my (2018).

A central premise in Condorcet's argument was the claim that arbitrary interference has some very specific consequences for the well-being of those who are subject to it. In the case of producers or manufacturers who are subject to potential visits by inspectors, this means that they are less likely to put any effort into any sort of innovation, as this effort might lead to loss, they are less likely to care about treating those who work for them justly, as the regulations might not lend themselves to equity, and they are less likely to develop virtuous traits as employers or citizens, because they cannot rely on being able to act according to their own judgement, so that any character trait they might have is on the whole irrelevant to the way in which they conduct their business.

Jean-Marie Roland de la Platière, who before he became Minister of the Interior during the revolution worked as the inspector of manufacturing, also observed first-hand the detrimental effects on the economy of government interference:

> I have looked in vain for the kind of manufacturing rules that we should have in place for the good of the trade, I have read them all, I have meditated on this cold and heavy compilation, I have envisaged the effects, and followed up their consequences. I think they should all be abolished. (1778, Reply to Necker's Survey, in Reynolds, 2013, 36)

Roland himself had witnessed factories being closed, equipment being confiscated, and individuals being bankrupted or put out of work for failing to comply with highly arbitrary and non-economically beneficial legislation. This led him to the conclusion that on the whole, the laws that regulated manufacturing, instead of benefiting production, slowed it down, and at the same time contributed to lowering the morale and ambition of those who might otherwise help to better the economy. In other words, his observations on manufacturing matched those of Condorcet and Turgot on the production of grain: the government's interference was merely a way of oppressing its subjects and reinforcing a politics of domination, and was in no way conducive to progress or development, whether economic or social. Given the importance that the price of bread and the conditions of life of the farmers who produced the flour had at the beginning of the revolution (the 1789 riots were in a sense a replay of the 1775 flour wars), it is no surprise that economic considerations should be central to Condorcet's political arguments.

Wollstonecraft, it seems, was a fan of Turgot, for very much the same reasons Condorcet was:

> On the eve of the American war, the enlightened administration of the comptroller general Turgot, a man formed in this school [the economists], afforded France a glimpse of freedom, which, streaking the horizon of despotism, only served to render the contrast more striking. Eager to correct abuses, equally impolitic and cruel, this most excellent man, suffering his clear judgment to be clouded by zeal, roused the nest of wasps [...] and he was obliged to retire from the office, which he so worthily filled. (1989, vol 6, 19)

In doing so, Wollstonecraft adds, he was 'disappointed in his noble plan of freeing France from fangs of despotism', and had he been allowed to go through with plan, 'the miseries of anarchy' might have been avoided and 'the empire of tyranny' might have been overcome instead by a 'revolution in opinion'. Turgot is praised a number of times in *View*, as often, nearly, as Jacques Necker, his replacement (and the father of Germaine de Staël), is mocked or condemned. She praises Turgot for his character (30, 42), his policies (19, 50), and his contributions to the *Encyclopedia* (226).

There are nearly thirty references to the price of bread, grain, and flour in *View*, but none relating to the bread riots of 1776, which were brought on in part by Turgot's policies. Wollstonecraft's various comments on bread shortages, notes Catherine Packham (2014, 710), display a certain 'coyness': she doesn't seem entirely confident that bread was in fact missing, that it was – or was not – as a result of a government plot, or that it was the real reason for the women's march to Versailles. In fact, she appears suspicious that the market women who walked down to Versailles to fetch the King back to Paris in the summer 1789 were self-motivated:

> That a body of women should put themselves in motion to demand relief of the king, or to remonstrate with the assembly respecting their tardy manner of forming the constitution is scarcely probable; and that they have undertaken the business, without being instigated by designing persons, when all Paris was dissatisfied with the conduct and procrastination of the assembly, is a belief which the most credulous will hardly swallow, unless they take into their view that the want of bread was the bye word used by those, who in a great measure produced it; for

perceiving the turn the public mind was taking, they drove the mob to perpetrate the mischief long designed, under the sanction of national indignation. (1989, vol 6, 207)

Twice before in the same chapter, Wollstonecraft attempts to cast doubt on the agency of the women who walked down to Versailles, suggesting they were infiltrated by men, dressed as women, who controlled the action. Here she is also asking us to consider whether the price of bread was a genuine motivation, or whether it was a pretext to invade Versailles. This is not a passage in which Wollstonecraft comes out looking good, either for her view of the motivation of the French people or her characterization of the market women. In 1791, she had taken on Edmund Burke for his insulting remarks about these very women, but after a few years in Paris, it seems she is happy to dismiss, if not insult them.

Politicians and Philosophers

Political realism, we saw, asks at very least that we let go of certain ideologies when devising political principles or actions. According to the first four tenets of Pettit's definition, realism ought to be anti-moralist, anti-deontologist, anti-transcendentalist, and anti-utopian. But this, we also saw in Mark Philp's discussion of Bernard Williams, doesn't mean that those who devise political principles or enact them ought to be free of moral or religious concerns, or have no desire to make the world better for everyone. In fact, there is no reason why politicians should not be informed by philosophers. Wollstonecraft, although she believed that the widespread reading of Rousseau among those who were not equipped to understand his works was to blame for some of the excesses of the French revolution (1989, vol 6, 61), also argued that it was the philosophical background of some of the actors who took the necessary steps to save the revolution and establish the republic by producing 'a simple code of instruction' that would educate citizens in political thought (221).

Still Wollstonecraft did not believe that politicians should be philosopher kings, and in *View*, she takes care to distinguish what she sees as the work specific to each:

> And, perhaps, it will appear just to separate the character of the philosopher, who dedicates his exertions to promote the welfare, and perfection

of mankind, carrying his views beyond any time he chooses to mark' from that of the politician, whose duty it is to attend to the improvement and interest of the time in which he lives, and not sacrifice any present comfort to a prospect of future perfection or happiness. (1989, vol 6, 154)

The philosopher must not stop developing ideals, and the politician must be informed by them. But the politician must act now, and look to the interests of those who form their constituency, before those of future citizens. This does not mean that the politician should not care about future generations or the future of the planet, but they should not prioritize this over immediate needs. These are not frivolous needs, such as the need to run cars and household machines that use up the earth's natural resources for the sake of a little extra comfort. But the politician might privilege reforming primary education over the opening of new universities. There is a natural order of things that needs to be observed, and that doesn't necessarily track what the philosopher might think matters most. This leads Wollstonecraft to make the following distinction, bringing the reader back to her discussion of human nature ten pages earlier in the book:

> If this definition be just, the philosopher naturally becomes a passive, the politician an active character. For though the desire of loudly proclaiming the grand principles of liberty to extend them quickly, be one of the most powerful a benevolent man, of every description of mind, feels; he no sooner wishes to obey this impulse, than he finds himself placed between two rocks. Truth commands him to say all; wisdom whispers to him to temporize. A love of justice would lead him to bound over these cautious restraints of prudence; did not humanity, enlightened by a knowledge of human nature, make him dread to purchase the good of posterity too dearly, by the misery of the present generation. (1989, vol 6, 154)

A politician does not lose track of what human beings are capable of, through their nature, and in whatever is their current state. Substituting ideals of justice for more prudent action would mean losing track of that, and forcing upon humanity the sort of course of action that will bring about 'the misery of the present generation'. More than anything, Wollstonecraft wants the politician to temporize. Nothing that happens quickly can last, because lasting change needs deep-rooted action, and that takes time (183). This is what Wollstonecraft tells us in the

Vindication of the Rights of Woman. As a philosopher, she says, 'my heart bounds with the anticipation of the general diffusion of that sublime contentment which only morality can diffuse' (209). But the rights of woman can only be established slowly, and 'who can tell', she asks, 'how many generations may be necessary to give vigour to the virtue and talents of the freed posterity of abject slaves?' (2014, 104).

Studying Wollstonecraft's work on the French Revolution teaches us how political philosophy can be applied. Appealing to the same principles she develops in her more theoretical works, Wollstonecraft criticizes the French reforms as they happen, offering her rich philosophical insights to an already very philosophical debate.

CHAPTER 8

Where Will the Men Go?

'Why Can't Women Be More like Men?'

In both her *Vindications*, as we saw, Wollstonecraft decries what she sees as the attributes of femininity: superficial emotions, fragility, physical weakness, dressing the body to appear less strong and more appealing. She sees these traits not just in upper- and middle-class women (lower-class women cannot afford to sacrifice their physical strength for the sake of looking pretty) but also in men. As Claudia Johnson wrote, 'Wollstonecraft has been seen as advocating masculinity in women; but the *Rights of Woman* is more striking for relentlessly savaging the femininity of Men' (Johnson 1995, 30). In fact, her first target is Burke himself, the author of *Reflections on the Revolution in France*, to whom she responds in her *Vindication of the Rights of Men*. She denounces 'the social arrangements Burke favors on the grounds that they are "effeminate" – craven, frivolous, enervated, irrational, voluptuous, given to frippery' (Johnson 1995, 30).

Boys who go to boarding schools, we also saw, acquire an 'effeminate' manner:

> But, on the contrary, when they are brought up at home, though they may pursue a plan of study in a more orderly manner than can be adopted when near a fourth part of the year is actually spent in idleness, and as much more in regret and anticipation; yet they there acquire too high an opinion of their own importance, from being allowed to tyrannize over servants, and from the anxiety expressed by most mothers, on the score of manners, who, eager to teach the accomplishments of a gentleman, stifle, in their birth, the virtues of a man. Thus brought

into company when they ought to be seriously employed, and treated like men when they are still boys, they become vain and effeminate. (Wollstonecraft 2014, 189)

This can be avoided simply by keeping boys at home and sending them to day schools, so that they are kept away from the tyranny of fashion that will prevent their character from developing. But for women, who are brought up from the start to embody 'submissive charms' (Wollstonecraft 2014, 59), femininity is much more likely to stick, and if they somehow manage to escape their destiny of weakness and beauty, they will be 'hunted out of society as masculine' (Wollstonecraft 2014, 60).

It makes sense, then, to read Wollstonecraft as saying that women should be masculine, but only if we think of masculinity as being not the attributes proper to men, but those proper to human beings in general. This fits in with the view which was put forward later by Simone de Beauvoir – that to be a man is considered the norm for humanity, and to be a woman is to be 'other'. If that is the case, then the virtues men claim for themselves are human virtues, while those which women are told are better suited for them are not: feminine traits are grown by 'stifling' human nature, that is, reason and the propensity for virtue. They are a degradation of humanity that is intended to render people submissive.

Wollstonecraft's critique of masculinity and femininity doesn't fit well with what we see in the world today. She doesn't seem to have much of a concept of what we call 'toxic masculinity', which may be in part because efforts to conform to masculine traits to the extreme may themselves be a consequence of a blurring of gender attributes which Wollstonecraft was hoping would happen. Men, seeing women behave more like them and become less submissive, want to retreat into a more extreme form of what they were in order to keep the difference – and sometimes their ascendance – alive. Nor could Wollstonecraft imagine the role that feminine manners and attire would play in a more gender-fluid society. The concept of a 'femme' in the LGBTI+ community, for instance, allows for greater expressions of gender and sexuality, and is detached from structures of gender oppression. To be a 'femme' lesbian does not mean that one is socially or politically submissive, and being 'butch' does not mean that one accesses more political rights (note: the term 'femme' is used outside the lesbian community – this is just an example).

Perhaps Wollstonecraft today would revise her view that to be masculine is the right way to be in the light of examples of toxic masculinity. And perhaps she would have concluded that there was a spectrum of ways to be that were neither dominating nor submissive. But in the context she is writing in, it is clear that when she says that she wishes neither men nor women to be feminine, she is referring to the propensity to sacrifice virtue and strength to superficial attractiveness. It is hard to disagree.

Do We Need Men at All?

In Virginie Despentes's novel *Cher Connard*, one of the protagonists, a young feminist activist blogging about the #metoo movement, asks herself whether a world without men was still something that could be contemplated. It is now possible, she sees, to breed women from women, and to create a world that is exclusively female. But if Valerie Solanas (who titled her manifesto SCUM, the acronym for 'Society for Cutting up Men') were to come back, she asks, and if she were to see that her dream was now a possibility, would she go for it? The blogger pauses: probably not. Even Solanas did not have the stomach for mass murder and the elimination of an entire gender. A world without men, the #metoo blogger realizes, was not something to work towards, but more of a metaphor for a world in which gender oppression did not happen.

Solanas, writing in the mid-1960s, explicitly rejected the idea of separationist feminism. To leave the men to their world and go and create a separate, women-only world would be to opt out, she thought:

> Most women are already dropped out; they were never in. Dropping out gives control to those few who don't drop out; dropping out is exactly what the establishment leaders want; it plays into the hands of the enemy; it strengthens the system instead of undermining it, since it is based entirely on the non-participation, passivity, apathy, and non-involvement of the mass of women. Dropping out, however, is an excellent policy for men and SCUM will enthusiastically encourage it. (Solanas 2004, 69–70)

Solanas does, of course, advocate violence towards men – as the name of her manifesto indicates – but even if this recommendation is to be read literally (and she did, after all, shoot Andy Warhol), it does not amount to eliminating all men. She plans on teaching some men to live in a woman-dominated society. Rose A. Owen, writing about SCUM, explains that Solanas advocated 'the feminist use of violence as a world-making activity' to be contrasted with the more pacificist impulse to drop out and start again. If we choose not to take her claims about actual physical violence seriously, we can think of her recommendation as a sort of 'revolution in manners'. And if we think that physical violence cannot be subtracted from her feminist theory, then we just need to remember that Wollstonecraft was a strong advocate of the French revolution.

The take-away message here is not that Valerie Solanas is the rightful heir to Wollstonecraft (although she may be one of them), but that the elimination of all men from society is not a solution that Wollstonecraft would have contemplated, for a reason similar to Solanas's: in order to become fully human, one must learn to live together, to share the world (the natural world, the political world, and the domestic world) and its works together.

The idea that women could live in a world that is free of men is also greatly complicated by the element of gender. In Sandra Newman's novel *The Men*, all human beings with a Y chromosome suddenly disappear, leaving a world inhabited by only those who have an X chromosome. But that's where the novel doesn't work: eliminating Y chromosomes won't eliminate men: it won't eliminate those with chromosome anomalies, and it won't eliminate transmen. Some have seen this omission in the novel as a sign that some feminist views need to be updated. We can also see in it the error of attempting to reduce patriarchal oppression to a chromosomal difference: X and Y don't account for the multiple levels of domination and inequality that make up gender relations, even for Wollstonecraft. Wollstonecraft is not a separatist feminist because she has (as we saw in early chapters) a rich multilayered conception of oppression which does not attach itself to chromosomal difference.

A Good Male Role Model

It is quite common to hear, of children brought up by single mothers or lesbian couples, that they are in need of 'a good male role model'. Conversely, a child brought up by a single father will be expected to lack a 'soft motherly touch' in his life. Does this mean society at large still perceives men and women as essentially different, and that a feminist taking after Wollstonecraft would want to eliminate the very idea of a 'male role model'? Rosanna Hertz, in a study of single motherhood, writes:

> Men and masculinity become a piece of cultural capital offered up to children as an additional resource, not an essential component. Ironically, the fact that women seek out men as a form of cultural capital reinforces the very gender ideology that they hope to displace in raising their children. (Hertz 2006, 188)

In other words, there is a disturbing double standard at play: women don't need men to thrive, but children (male or female) do. Is there a way to reconcile women's independence and this perceived need for children to have men in their lives?

A social media conversation about whether looking for men or male role models for the children of single mothers was an attempt to fit in with the patriarchy brought up interesting answers. I found out that some people seek out men or male role models to make sure their child is exposed to what we might call non-toxic masculinity. As one friend put it, the drive to find such a role model for a son, in particular, might just be: 'We need to catch him before he starts watching Andrew Tate videos.' One philosopher offered an answer that I felt got it as close to right as I could hope for. Children need role models that expose them to the rich variety that human life can take, so not just 'men' or 'male'. But given the sheer number of men or males in the world, it is reasonable to want them to be well represented when we try to model human living for them.

Increasingly, a world without men will mean a world without the rich palette of genders that we now see. Sure, some cis-men are obstacles to the flourishing of individuals who are non-gender-conforming, or simply the wrong gender (F). But we can't offer a philosophical justification for taking out these individuals (or at least, I'm not willing to try!). But any decision to exclude men from society, whether through genetic engineering or outright genocide, would also seriously limit the gender spectrum: we could end up with a world, as in Sandra Newman's novel, populated only with cis-women. This is a step backwards in the evolution of gender.

What is the alternative? What do we do about the men who make rules that enforce binary gender norms, prevent women from living fulfilling lives and accessing the same opportunities as men, and prevent non-binary or trans people from living their lives at all? Wollstonecraft's answer would be to educate them. Teach people of all genders to live together, to recognize each other's humanity, habituate them to each other from the youngest possible age, so that they will not learn to think of each other as alien. This is exactly what is being prevented in parts of the world where all talk of gender is banned from schools, or where children are made to conform to certain norms – boys wear shorts, girls wear skirts, boys and girls play different sports – and where, when a non-gender-conforming child happens just to be there, the adults in charge, teachers, and parent groups instead of supporting them work towards their exclusion.

How to Speak to Men about Women?

In most of her work Mary Wollstonecraft addresses men. In the early educational works, she is addressing educators, that is, some men as well as women. In the *Historical and Moral View of the French Revolution*, she talks about women to men, sometimes making harsh and sexist comments about them. In the *Vindication of the Rights of Men*, she is addressing Burke, and in the *Letters from Denmark*, Imlay. This is a very standard way of writing in the eighteenth century. Men are the general audience, and women can be addressed when something concerns them specifically (so Rousseau, for instance, advised unmarried women not to read his *New Heloise*, which resulted in all of them buying it). We might expect the *Vindication of the Rights of Women* to be different. It is, after all, a work designed to change the way women live. But even in this case, the intended audience seems to be men more than women. Wollstonecraft addresses men directly on several occasions – as husbands and fathers – with no distinction of class or profession, but she specifies which category of women (i.e. middle class) are her intended audience. The rationale might be something like this: women cannot by themselves break their chains – they need the help of their captors, that is, men. So it makes sense to attempt to convince said captors that women need to be educated and transformed from decorative but useless (or worse, interfering) creatures into active citizens.

> Would men but generously snap our chains, and be content with rational fellowship instead of slavish obedience, they would find us more observant daughters, more affectionate sisters, more faithful wives, more reasonable mothers – in a word, better citizens. We should then love them with true affection, because we should learn to respect ourselves; and the peace of mind of a worthy man would not be interrupted by the idle vanity of his wife, nor the babes sent to nestle in a strange bosom, having never found a home in their mother's. (Wollstonecraft 2014, 179)

Note that this isn't the only way to proceed: Olympe de Gouges, in her *Declaration of the Rights of Woman*, addresses women, admonishing them to wake up, and, in her preface, she addresses the Queen, Marie-Antoinette, suggesting that she could still save herself if only she took up the cause of women for the revolution. But Wollstonecraft is writing in and for a conservative England, while Gouges is in the midst of a revolution.

So given that Wollstonecraft must address men, how should she address them? Her tone is sometimes harsh and mocking, earning her the moniker 'hyena in petticoats'. But she also knows how to pander to her audience. Men's superiority – at least, their physical strength – is underlined in the second *Vindication* (2014, 32, 65, 66). We saw in Chapter 4 (p. 61) that it's possible, even likely, that Wollstonecraft was not entirely sincere in her attribution of physical superiority to men. Women, she thinks, are weakened by a lack of fresh air and exercise and a very sedated lifestyle. But if she wants to get men on her side, and if she wants them to concede that as far as reason and virtue are concerned women are their equals and should be appropriately educated and allowed to participate in civic and political life, then she needs to concede something in exchange. Her proposal – civic and political equality, and the reform of gender relationships – is quite threatening to those who mostly benefit from the current state of affairs. Assuring men that they remain superior, even if only in bodily strength, is quite a good move in that sense. But it is pandering, or flattering, and perhaps not what one would expect from a writer as honest as Wollstonecraft.

One would like Wollstonecraft not to pander to her men readers. But she is having to navigate the waters between this and the tone police. Given that she was known as the 'hyena in petticoats', it's likely she was aware of how easily her arguments could be dismissed if she sounded a little too 'shrill'. She could not, as Valerie Solanas did just under two centuries later, insist on addressing men as 'turd'. This would not have resulted in the sort of support she was hoping for.

WWWD (What Would Wollstonecraft Do)?

Wollstonecraft was hopeful that equality between men and women would eventually arise out of education reform: and it seems she was at least partly right. In several parts of the world, men and women are able to interact with one another as equals – socially, intellectually, and politically. This is not yet as widespread as it ought to be, but it's certainly progress from eighteenth-century Europe.

Unfortunately, if the gender oppression that Wollstonecraft was fighting has somewhat diminished (though much work still needs to be done), whatever has been eliminated has been replaced by other forms of gender oppression, for example that of non-gender-conforming individuals. So has progress been made? Can we expect the sort of slow progress that cis-women fought for and benefited from for trans people? Especially given that cis-women themselves contribute to their oppression? Wollstonecraft was well aware that freeing white women from dependence on their husbands or fathers would only constitute one step towards eradicating oppression from humanity. She also wanted us to fight class and racial oppression. She would not be defeated, I think, by the new forms of gender oppressions we are witnessing. She'd pick up the fight where she'd left it.

References

Adams, Joseph. 1816. 'On Midwives and Accoucheurs'. *London Medical and Physical Journal, February*, 35(204): 84–88.
Affeldt, Steven G. 1999. 'The Force of Freedom: Rousseau on Forcing to Be Free'. *Political Theory*, 27(3): 299–333.
Astell, Mary. 2015. *Some Reflections upon Marriage*. Introduction by John A. Dussinger. Champaign: University of Illinois Press
Austen, Jane. 1997. *Mansfield Park*. New York: Norton.
Beauvoir, Simone de. 1965. *The Prime of Life*. Translated by Peter Green. London: Penguin.
Beauvoir, Simone de. 2006. *She Came to Stay*. Translated by Yvonne Moise, Roger Senhouse. London: Harper Press.
Beauvoir, Simone de. 2009. *The Second Sex*, translated by Constance Borde and Sheila Malovany-Chevallier. Vintage E-book.
Bergès. 2011. 'Why Women Hug their Chains: Wollstonecraft and Adaptive Preferences'. *Utilitas*, 23: 72–87.
Bergès, Sandrine. 2013a. *Mothers and Independent Citizens: Making Sense of Wollstonecraft's Supposed Essentialism*. Philosophical Papers, 42(3): 259–284.
Bergès, Sandrine. 2013b. *Routledge Guidebook to the Vindication of the Rights of Woman*. London: Routledge.
Bergès, Sandrine. 2016. 'A Republican Housewife: Marie-Jeanne Phlipon Roland on Women's Political Role'. *Hypatia*, 31: 107–122, 112.
Bergès, Sandrine. 2018. 'What's It Got to Do with the Price of Bread? Condorcet and Grouchy on Freedom and Unreasonable Laws in Commerce'. *European Journal of Political Theory*, 17(4): 432–448.
Bergès, Sandrine. 2019. 'Wollstonecraft'. In *A Companion to Atheism and Philosophy*, Graham Oppy (ed), Chichester: Wiley, pp. 58–70.
Bergès, Sandrine. 2022a. *Olympe de Gouges*. Cambridge: Cambridge University Press.
Bergès, Sandrine. 2022b. *Liberty in their Names*. London; Bloomsbury.

Bergès, Sandrine. 2024. 'Mary Wollstonecraft's Influence on French Revolutionary Educational Reform' Women's Writings. https://doi.org/10.1080/09699082.2024.2360616.
Bergès, Sandrine, Botting, Eileen Hunt and Coffee, Alan (Eds). 2019. *The Wollstonecraftian Mind*. Abington: Routlege.
Botting, Eileen Hunt. 2016. *Wollstonecraft, Mill and Women's Human Rights*. New Haven: Yale University Press. (on rights and Kant) 31.
Botting, Eileen Hunt. 2021. 'Wollstonecraft in Jamaica: The International Reception of a Vindication of the Rights of Men in the Kingston Daily Advertiser in 1791'. *History of European Ideas*, 47(8): 1304–1314.
Bour, Isabelle. 2022. 'Who Translated into French and Annotated Mary Wollstonecraft's *Vindication of the Rights of Woman?*' *History of European Ideas*, 48(7): 879–891.
Brace, Laura. 2000. '"Not Empire, but Equality": Mary Wollstonecraft, the Marriage State and the Sexual Contract'. *The Journal of Political Philosophy*, 8(4): 433–455.
Bracewell, Lorna. 2019. 'Gender and Social Theory in Mary Wollstonecraft's Thought'. In Berges, Botting and Coffee (eds), pp. 476–488.
Bradford, Helen. 1996. 'Women, Gender and Colonialism: Rethinking the History of the British Cape Colony and Its Frontier Zones, C. 1806–70'. *The Journal of African History*, 37(3), 351–370. www.jstor.org/stable/182498.
Bugg, John. 2006. 'The Other Interesting Narrative: Olaudah Equiano's Public Book Tour'. *PMLA*, 121(5): 1424–1442.
Burgh, James. 1747. *Thoughts on Education*. London.
Burke, Edmund. 1986. *Reflections on the Revolution in France*. Hammondsworth: Penguin.
Cahill, Samara Ann. 2019. *Intelligent Souls? Feminist Orientalism in Eighteenth-Century English Literatures*. Lewisburg: Bucknell University Press.
Carroll, Ross. 2019. 'Epistolary and Travel Writings'. In Bergès, Botting, and Coffee, pp. 145–158.
Clough, Sharyn. 2011. 'Gender and the Hygiene Hypothesis'. *Social Science and Medicine*, 72: 486–493.
Cobbe, Frances Power. 1995. 'The Subjection of Women'. In *The Subjection of Women*, A. Pyle (ed), Bristol: Thoemmes Press, pp. 54–74.
Coffee, Alan. 2018. 'Independence or Non-domination as Relational Freedom: A Relational Account of Republican Freedom Derived from Mary Wollstonecraft'. In *Women Philosophers on Autonomy*, Sandrine Berges and Alberto Siani (eds), London: Routledge, pp. 94–112.
Condorcet, Nicolas de. 2012. *Political Writings*. Edited by Steven Lukes and Nadia Urbinati. Cambridge: Cambridge University Press.

Cooper, Christine M. 2004. 'Reading the Politics of Abortion: Mary Wollstonecraft Revisited'. *Eighteenth-Century Fiction*, 16(4): 735–782.

Craciun, Adriana. 2002. *Mary Wollstonecraft's a Vindication of the Rights of Woman, a Sourcebook*. London: Routledge.

Craciun, Adriana. 2003. *Fatal Women of Romanticism*. Cambridge: Cambridge University Press.

Criado-Perez, Caroline. 2019. *Invisible Women*. London: Chatto & Windus

Despentes, Virginie. 2022. *Cher Connard*. Paris: Grasset.

Donington, Katie. 2020. 'Slavery and Abolition'. In *Mary Wollstonecraft in Context*, Nancy E. Johnson and Paul Keen (eds), Cambridge: Cambridge University Press, pp. 222–229.

Du Bois, W. E. B. 2014. *The Autobiography of W.E.B Du Bois*. New York: Oxford University Press.

Dutsch, Dorotha. 2020. *Pythagorean Women Philosophers, between Belief and Suspicion* New York: Oxford University Press.

Edelman-Young, Diana. 2014. 'Chubby Cheeks and the Bloated Monster: The Politics of Reproduction in Mary Wollstonecraft's *Vindication*'. *European Romantic Review*, 25(6): 683–704.

Eichner, Carolyn J. 2009. '*La Citoyenne* in the World: Hubertine Auclert and Feminist Imperialism'. *French Historical Studies*, 32(1): 63–84.

Eknoyan, Garabed. 2006. 'A History of Obesity, or How What Was Good Became Ugly and Then Bad'. *Advances in Chronic Kidney Disease*, 13(4): 421–427.

Eliot, George. 1855. "Margaret Fuller and Mary Wollstonecraft." *The Leader*, 13 October 1855, VI(290): 988–989.

Erickson, Amy Louise. 2008. 'Clockmakers, Milliners and Mistresses: Women Trading in the City of London Companies 1700–1750' www.campop.geog.cam.ac.uk/research/occupations/outputs/preliminary/paper16.pdf.

Federici, Silvia. 1975. *Wages against Housework*. Bristol: Falling Wall Press.

Fergusson, Moira. 1992. 'Mary Wollstonecraft and the Problem of Slavery'. *Feminist Review* 42: 82–102.

Ford, Thomas H. 2009. 'Mary Wollstonecraft and the Motherhood of Feminism'. *Women's Studies Quarterly*, 37(3/4): 189–205. 190.

Forestié, Edouard. 1901. *Olympe de Gouges* printed by the author in Montauban.

Frazer, Antonia, 2021. *The Case of the Married Woman: Caroline Norton: A 19th Century Heroine Who Wanted Justice for Women*. London: Weidenfeld & Nicolson.

Frye, Marilyn. 2000. 'Oppression'. In *Gender Basics: Feminist Perspectives on Women and Men*, Anna Minas (ed), 2nd ed. Belmont: Wadsworth, pp. 10–16.

Garcia, Manon, 2018. *On ne Nait pas Soumise, on le Devient*. Paris: Flammarion.

Geuss, Raymond, 2009. *Philosophy and Real Politics*. Princeton: Princeton University Press.
Gheaus, Anca. 2008. 'Basic Income, Gender Justice and the Costs of Gender-symmetrical Lifestyles'. *Basic Income Studies*, 3(3): 1–8.
Gheaus, Anca. 2021. 'Child-Rearing with Minimal Domination: A Republican Account'. *Political Studies*, 69(3): 748–766.
Gilman Sander, L. 2017. 'The Fat Person on the Edgware Road Omnibus: Fat, Fashion, and Public Shaming in the British Long Eighteenth Century'. Lit Med., 35(2): 431–447.
Graeber, David, and Wengrow, David. 2021. *The Dawn of Everything: A New Story of Humanity*. Toronto: Penguin Random House Canada.
Gutwirth. Madelyn. 2004. 'Suzanne Necker's Legacy: Breastfeeding as Metonym'. *Eighteenth-Century Life*, 28(2): 19–20.
Halldenius, Lena. 2015. *Mary Wollstonecraft and Feminist Republicanism*. London: Routledge.
Haslam, David, and Haslam, Fiona. 2009. *Fat, Gluttony and Sloth: Obesity in Literature, Art and Medicine*. Liverpool: Liverpool University Press.
Hay, Carol. 2020. *Think like a Feminist*. New York: Norton.
Hay, Daisy. 2022. *Dinner with Joseph Johnson*. Princeton: Princeton University Press.
Hertz, Rosanna. 2006. 'A World without Men, Amen?'. In *Single by Chance, Mothers by Choice: How Women are Choosing Parenthood without Marriage and Creating the New American Family*. Oxford: Oxford University Press, pp. 177–189.
Hont, Istvan. 2006. 'The Early Enlightenment Debate on Commerce and Luxury'. In *The Cambridge History of Eighteenth-Century Political Thought*, Mark Goldie and Robert Wokler (eds), Cambridge: Cambridge University Press, pp. 377–418.
Hursthouse, Rosalind. 1991. 'Virtue Theory and Abortion'. *Philosophy & Public Affairs*, 20(3): 223–246.
Jacobus, Mary. 1992. 'Incorruptible Milk: Breastfeeding and the French Revolution'. In *Rebel Daughters: Women and the French Revolution*, Sarah E. Melzer and Leslie W. Rabine (eds), New York: Oxford University Press, pp. 54–78.
James, David. 2013. *Rousseau and German Idealism: Freedom, Dependence and Necessity*. Cambridge: Cambridge University Press.
Johnson, Claudia. 1995. *Equivocal Beings: Politics, Gender, and Sentimentality in the 1790s–Wollstonecraft, Radcliffe, Burney, Austen*. Chicago: The University of Chicago Press.
Kant, Immanuel. 2012. *Groundwork of the Metaphysics of Morals*. Cambridge: Cambridge University Press.

Khader, Serene. 2012. 'Must Theorizing about Adaptive Preferences Deny Women's Agency?' *Journal of Applied Philosophy*, 29(4): 302–317.

Khader, Serene. 2015. 'Development Ethics, Gender Complementarianism, and Intrahousehold Inequality'. *Hypatia*, 30(2): 352–369.

Khader, Serene. 2017. 'Transnational Feminisms, Nonideal Theory, and "Other" Women's Power'. *Feminist Philosophy Quarterly*, 3: 1

Kirkpatrick, Kate. 2019. *Becoming Beauvoir*. London: Bloomsbury.

Knowles, Charlotte. 2020. 'Philosophy and the Maternal'. *Studies in the Maternal*, 13(1): 1–8.

Knowles, Charlotte. 2021. 'Beyond Adaptive Preferences. Rethinking Women's Complicity in their Own Subordination'. *European Journal of Philosophy*. 30 (4): 1317–1334.

Knowles, John. 1881. *Life and Writings of Henry Fuseli*, Vol 1. London: Henry Colburn and Richard Bentley.

Le Doeuff, Michelle. 2003. *Sex of Knowing*. New York: Routledge.

Lefebvre, Alexandre. 2019. 'Human Rights'. In Bergès, Botting, and Coffee, pp. 429–440.

Leo, Maya del. 2021. *Queer. Storia culturale della comunità LGBT+*. Turin: Finaudi.

Levitan, William, trans. 2007. *Abelard and Heloise, The Letters and Other Writings*. Indianapolis: Hacket.

Macaulay, Catharine. 2014. *Letters on Education: With Observations on Religious and Metaphysical Subjects*. Cambridge: Cambridge University Press.

Moi, Toril. 2008. *Simone de Beauvoir: The Making of an Intellectual Woman*. Oxford: Oxford University Press.

Murray, Julie. 2020. '1970s Critical Reception'. In *Mary Wollstonecraft in Context*, Nancy Johnson and Paul Keen (eds), Cambridge: Cambridge University Press, 57–63.

Myers, Mitzi. 1982, 'Reform or Ruin: "A Revolution in Female Manners"'. *Studies in Eighteenth-Century Culture*, 11: 199–216.

1988. 'Pedagogy as Self-Expression in Mary Wollstonecraft: Exorcising the Past, Finding a Voice'. In *The Private Self: Theory and Practice of Women's Autobiographical Writings*. Shari Benstock (ed). Chapel Hill: University of North Carolina Press, 192–210.

Newman Sandra. 2022. *The Men*. London: Granta Books.

O'Neill, Eileen. 1997. 'History of Philosophy: Disappearing Ink: Early Modern Women Philosophers and Their Fate in History'. *Philosophy in a Feminist Voice: Critiques and Reconstructions*, Janet A. Kourany (ed), Princeton: Princeton University Press, pp. 17–62.

Offen, Karen. 1988. 'On the French Origin of the Words Feminism and Feminist'. *Feminist Issues*, 8(2): 45–51.

Packham, Catherine. 2014. '"The Common Grievance of the Revolution": Bread, the Grain Trade, and Political Economy in Wollstonecraft's View of the French Revolution'. *European Romantic Review*, 25(6): 705–722.
Packham, Catherine. 2024. *Mary Wollstonecraft and Political Economy*. Cambridge: Cambridge University Press.
Pettit, Phili. 2017. 'Political Realism Meets Civic Republicanism'. *Critical Review of International Social and Political Philosophy*, 20(3): 331–347.
Philp, Mark. 2012. 'Realism without Illusions'. *Political Theory*, 40(5): 629–649.
Pizan, Christine de. 1982. *The Book of the City of Ladies*. Translated by Earl Jeffrey Richards. New York: Persea Books.
Prince, Mary. 1831. *The History of Mary Prince, a West Indian Slave, Related by Herself*. London: Westley and Davis.
Pyle, Andrew. 1995. *The Subjection of Women*. Bristol: Thoemmes Press.
Reuter, Martina. 2022. *Mary Wollstonecraft*. Cambridge: Cambridge University Press.
Reynolds, Sian. 2012. *Marriage and Revolution*. Oxford: Oxford University Press.
Rousseau, Jean-Jacques. 1765. *Constitutional Project for Corsica*. Edinburgh: Thomas Nelson and Sons ltd.
Rousseau, Jean-Jacques. 1979. *Emile, or on Education*. Trans. Allan Bloom. New York: Basic Books.
Rousseau, Jean-Jacques. 1997. *Julie, or the New Heloise*. Trans. and annotated by Philip Stewart and Jean Vache. Lebanon: University Press of New England.
Rousseau, Jean-Jacques. 2018. *Rousseau: The Discourses and Other Early Political Writings*. 2nd ed. *Cambridge Texts in the History of Political Thought*, Victor Gourevitch (ed), Cambridge: Cambridge University Press.
Sagar Rahul, and Andrew Sabl. 2018. *Realism in Political Theory*. Abingdon: Routledge.
Sapiro, Virginia. 1992. *Vindication of the Rights of Virtue*. Chicago: University of Chicago Press.
Sartre. 2018. *Being and Nothingness*. Tr. Sarah Richmond. New York: Washington Square Press.
Sawbridge David, and Fitzgerald, Richard. 2009. '"Lazy, Slothful and Indolent": Medical and Social Perceptions of Obesity in Europe to the Eighteenth Century'. *Vesalius*, 15(2): 59–70.
Sen, Amartya. 1992. *Inequality Re-examined*. Cambridge, MA: Harvard University Press.
Sen, Amartya. 2006. 'Reason, Freedom, and Well-Being'. *Utilitas* 18: 80–86.

Sen, Amartya. 2005. 'Mary, Mary, Quite Contrary!' *Feminist Economics*, 11(1): 1–9.
Sen, Amartya. 2011. *The Idea of Justice*. Cambridge, MA: Belknap Press of Harvard University Press.
Sheridan, Bridgette Ann. 2011. '"Her Lack of Capacity Makes Her Wise and Circumspect": Echoes of the *Querelle des Femmes* in Midwifery Debates in Early Eighteenth-Century France'. *Journal of the Western Society for French History*, 39: 53–64.
Solanas, Valerie. 2004. *SCUM Manifesto*. London: Verso.
Stanton, Donna C., and Rebecca M. Wilkin, eds. and trans. 2010. *Gabrielle Suchon, a Woman Who Defends All the Persons of Her Sex: Selected Philosophical and Moral Writings*. The Other Voice in Early Modern Europe series. Chicago: University of Chicago Press.
Strings, Sabrina. 2019. *Fearing the Black Body: The Racial Origins of Fat Phobia*. New York: New York University Press.
Szreter, Simon, and Siena, Kevin. 2021. 'The Pox in Boswell's London: An Estimate of the Extent of Syphilis Infection in the Metropolis in the 1770s'. *The Economic History Review*, 74: 372–399.
Tomaselli, Sylvana. 2020. *Wollstonecraft: Philosophy, Passion and Politics*. Princeton: Princeton University Press.
Truth, Sojourner. 1851. 'Akron Speech, Reprinted'. In *The Penguin Book of Feminism*, Hannah Dawson (ed), London: Penguin, pp. 42–43.
UN DESA, & Gapminder. (June 17, 2019). Life Expectancy (from Birth) in the United Kingdom from 1765 to 2020* [Graph]. In *Statista*. May 16, 2024, www.statista.com/statistics/1040159/life-expectancy-united-kingdom-all-time/.
Verges, Francoise. 2021. *A Decolonial Feminism*. London: Pluto Press.
Verhoeven, Wil. 2006. 'Gilbert Imlay and the Triangular Trade'. *The William and Mary Quarterly*, 63(4): 827–842.
Waters, Mary. 2004. '"The First of a New Genus —": Mary Wollstonecraft, Mary Hays, and *The Analytical Review*'. In *British Women Writers and the Profession of Literary Criticism, 1789–1832*, Mary Waters (ed). London: Palgrave Macmillan, pp. 86–120.
Williams, Bernard. 2005. 'Realism and Moralism in Political Theory'. In *In the Beginning Was the Deed*, Geoffrey Hawthorne (ed). Princeton: Princeton University Press, pp. 1–17.
Wilson, Adrian. 1995. *The Making of Man-Midwifery: Childbirth in England, 1660–1770*. London: Routledge.
Wollstonecraft, Mary. 1979. *Collected Letters*, edited by Ralph Wardle, Ithaca: Cornell University Press.
Wollstonecraft, Mary. 1989. *The Works of Mary Wollstonecraft*, 7 vols, Janet Todd and Marilyn Butler (eds), London: William Pickering.

Wollstonecraft, Mary. 2014. *Vindication of the Rights of Woman*. Edited by Eileen Hunt Botting. New Haven: Yale University Press.
Yorke-Edwards, Victoria. 2019. 'Obesity in London 1700–1850: The Evidence', PhD thesis presented at UCL 2019.
Young, Iris Marion. 1995. 'Mothers, Citizenship, and Independence: A Critique of Pure Family Values'. *Ethics*, 105: 535–556.
Young, Iris Marion. 1990. *Throwing Like a Girl and Other Essays in Feminist Philosophy and Social Theory*. Bloomington: Indiana University Press.
Zakaria, Rafia. 2021. *Against White Feminism*. London: Penguin

Index

A Moral and Historical View of the French Revolution, 5
abolitionism, 28
abortion, 7, 16, 72, 76, 77, 78, 79, 86
Analytical Review, 5
animals, 11
aristocrats, 9, 23, 25, 29, 32, 39, 41, 53, 68, 70, 74, 98, 126
Astell, Mary, 98, 100, 109
Atwood, Margaret, 70
Auclerc, Hubertine, 7
Austen, Jane, 54

bad faith, 56, *See* self-deception
Beauvoir, Simone de, 33
birdcage. *See* cage
bodies, 26, 35, 36, 59, 61, 62, 63, 68, 73, 74
bodily strength, 36, 62, 63, 141
boys, 13, 62, 63, 64, 65, 67, 68, 72, 82, 94, 95, 101, 121, 135, 139
Brissot, Jacques Pierre, 1
Burgh, James, 4
business, 40, 43, 91, 109, 110, 126, 129, 130

cage, 48
capacities, 12
capacity, 15, 20, 52, 54, 78, 89, 93, 118
Carrie, 81, 82
character, 25, 33, 54, 67, 71, 82, 89, 91, 111, 112, 115, 122, 127, 129, 130, 131, 132, 135
child, 4, 5, 11, 17, 26, 28, 35, 40, 41, 43, 48, 59, 66, 68, 72, 73, 74, 75, 76, 78, 80, 81, 82, 83, 84, 85, 86, 87, 88, 89, 90, 91, 92, 96, 97, 101, 103, 110, 112, 126, 138, 139
childbirth, 4
children, 1, 3, 4, 11, 15, 17, 24, 26, 34, 35, 36, 41, 42, 53, 57, 61, 64, 65, 67, 70, 72, 73, 74, 75, 76, 78, 80, 81, 82, 83, 84, 85, 86, 87, 88, 89, 90, 91, 92, 93, 96, 98, 101, 110, 111, 121, 122, 138, 139
class, 2, 3, 14, 16, 17, 22, 23, 24, 25, 26, 28, 37, 46, 51, 61, 63, 69, 70, 73, 81, 82, 92, 96, 97, 100, 101, 102, 110, 112, 114, 122, 134, 139, 141
commerce, 126, 127, 128
commercial, 69, 126, 127
commercialism, 127
compassion, 76, 77, 78
complementarism, 53
Condorcet, Nicolas de, 1
contraception, 72, 86, 92
Crocker, Hannah Mather, 93

daughters, 1, 6, 10, 49, 81, 87, 90, 98, 112, 140
decolonialism, 27
dependence, 58
dependent, 2, 15, 26, 42, 50, 80, 81, 103, 106, 107, 108, 110, 111, 112
deprivation, 56
Despentes, Virginie, 7
dolls, 34, 63
domination, 39, 57, 80, 81, 82, 83, 84, 86, 87, 88, 114, 125, 129, 137

education, 1, 3, 4, 10, 13, 17, 24, 25, 32, 33, 34, 36, 39, 40, 42, 46, 49, 61, 63, 66, 67, 69, 70, 71, 72, 73, 78, 80, 81, 83, 84, 85, 92, 93, 94, 96, 97, 98, 100, 101, 102, 106, 114, 119, 120, 121, 122, 124, 125, 132, 141
Eliza, 3, 43, 103, 104, 105, 107
Emile, 10, 40, 74, 93, 94, 96, 106
Eon, Madame d', 36, 69,
equality, 2, 7, 9, 65, 66, 91, 110, 111, 114, 140, 141
essentialism, 33
Everina, 3, 5, 39, 104, 105, 107

150

Index

exercise, 10, 13, 29, 42, 45, 54, 61, 63, 80, 84, 86, 93, 98, 119, 121, 140

family, 3, 6, 12, 24, 27, 31, 35, 37, 39, 40, 43, 47, 67, 74, 75, 81, 86, 90, 91, 92, 97, 98, 104, 107, 108, 112, 126
Fanny, 3, 5, 24, 35, 36, 49, 73, 88, 90, 92, 107, 112, 126, *See* Fanny Blood
Fanny Blood, 3
fathers, 10, 17, 24, 34, 35, 47, 73, 75, 80, 89, 90, 91, 92, 96, 101, 139, 141
feminism, 1, 2, 3, 6, 7, 8, 14, 16, 17, 19, 26, 27, 37, 51, 54, 64, 66, 67, 70, 71, 136, 137, 138
freedom, 20, 26, 27, 29, 30, 37, 41, 42, 44, 47, 48, 54, 56, 57, 58, 59, 81, 105, 123, 125, 127, 130
French Revolution, 1, 18, 25, 26, 74, 94, 109, 118, 123, 127, 139

gender, 8, 16, 18, 27, 33, 34, 36, 37, 51, 53, 65, 66, 68, 69, 106, 108, 111, 112, 114, 135, 136, 137, 138, 139, 140, 141
girls, 3, 10, 13, 36, 63, 64, 65, 66, 68, 72, 93, 94, 95, 96, 101, 121, 139
Godwin, William, 1
Gouges, Olympe de, 10

Haitian Revolution, 31
happiness, 13, 32, 116, 122, 123, 124, 126, 132
health, 4, 13, 16, 25, 35, 42, 44, 46, 47, 52, 62, 64, 65, 66, 75, 83, 110
hereditary power, 46
Historical and Moral View of the Origin and Progress of the French Revolution, 118
home, 3, 5, 17, 22, 25, 35, 47, 66, 67, 70, 72, 74, 77, 84, 85, 90, 91, 92, 95, 96, 98, 106, 107, 108, 109, 110, 119, 127, 134, 135, 140
housewife, 56, 106, 107
human, 1, 2, 6, 8, 9, 10, 11, 12, 13, 15, 22, 27, 32, 34, 52, 53, 57, 58, 63, 67, 68, 71, 78, 80, 81, 83, 84, 86, 95, 105, 114, 115, 116, 117, 123, 124, 126, 132, 135, 137, 138
human rights. *See* rights
husband, 1, 5, 6, 11, 12, 17, 21, 25, 31, 36, 40, 42, 43, 47, 48, 49, 50, 52, 54, 57, 72, 80, 86, 92, 94, 97, 98, 104, 109, 110, 111, 112

Imlay, Gilbert, 5
independence, 9, 17, 23, 41, 42, 43, 44, 45, 48, 49, 52, 58, 78, 91, 96, 102, 103, 105, 107, 109, 110, 125, 138
inequality, 51, 59, 62, 90, 92, 110, 114, 117, 137

institutions, 50
intersectionality, 22
Islam, 32

Johnson, Joseph, 5

Khader, Serene, 52
knowledge, 16, 64, 73, 75, 111, 117, 118, 120, 121, 123, 125, 132

laws, 50
Letters from Denmark, Sweden and Norway, 6
liberty, 2, 9, 25, 30, 44, 52, 81, 118, 119, 121, 122, 128, 132
luxury, 25

Macaulay, Catharine, 1
man, 12, 32, 37, 40, 41, 43, 44, 47, 50, 55, 56, 58, 63, 69, 70, 72, 77, 92, 95, 98, 100, 112, 118, 119, 120, 121, 126, 130, 132, 134, 135, 140
manipulation, 61, 119
manners, 9, 10, 11, 14, 16, 26, 34, 67, 68, 69, 71, 78, 81, 118, 134, 135, 137
Maria, or the Wrongs of Woman, 6
marriage, 17, 40, 41, 42, 43, 47, 49, 72, 79, 87, 95, 97, 98, 100, 103, 109, 111, 112
masculinity, 18
maternal duties, 72
men, 15, 18
middle class. *See* class
midwives, 99, 100
mis-education, 45, 61, 62, 65, 66
money, 24, 25, 39, 41, 42, 49, 69, 72, 103, 104, 106, 108, 109, 111, 126
morality, 12, 86, 115, 116, 118, 119, 122, 123, 124, 127, 133
motherhood, 22, 34, 35, 57, 70, 71, 72, 110, 138
mothers, 10, 17, 34, 35, 66, 72, 73, 74, 75, 80, 89, 90, 91, 93, 96, 102, 106, 110, 134, 138, 140

Newington Green, 3
nursery, 72, 91

O'Neill, Eileen, 21
oppression, 14

Paine, Thomas, 1
parental domination, 17, 83
parenting, 17, 73, 74, 87, 89, 90, 91, 92, 113

parents, 4, 17, 35, 40, 46, 58, 65, 66, 67, 69, 71, 72, 73, 74, 76, 78, 80, 81, 82, 83, 84, 85, 86, 87, 88, 89, 90, 91, 139
patriarchy, 15
perfectible, 114
philosophers, 8, 21, 100, 115
philosophy, 2, 3, 8, 16, 17, 21, 38, 57, 65, 71, 95, 98, 107, 114, 116, 121, 124, 125, 127
physical strength, 16
play, 35, 46, 53, 54, 59, 63, 64, 66, 73, 76, 82, 83, 88, 101, 107, 118, 125, 135, 138, 139
pleasure, 32, 50, 51, 75, 78, 110
political philosophy, 2
politics, 3, 100, 102, 115, 116, 121, 122, 124, 128, 129
poverty, 24
pregnancy, 77
pregnant, 4, 5, 35, 43, 73, 76, 77, 79, 103, 104, 126
prejudice, 13
Price, Richard, 1
Prince, Mary, 37
professions, 100, 103
progress, 2, 5, 13, 18, 34, 37, 67, 85, 88, 89, 99, 115, 117, 118, 120, 121, 122, 123, 124, 129, 141
prostitution, 40

racism, 16, 23, 27, 31, 62, 102
rape, 27, 76, 77, 79
Rational Dissenters, 1, 4
realism, 114, 115, 116, 131
reason, 2, 8, 9, 10, 12, 14, 15, 16, 17, 18, 21, 32, 33, 35, 36, 38, 44, 45, 46, 47, 48, 50, 54, 61, 62, 66, 80, 83, 84, 85, 86, 87, 88, 89, 91, 92, 93, 99, 102, 104, 108, 110, 111, 112, 114, 118, 119, 120, 121, 123, 124, 125, 130, 131, 135, 137, 140
religion, 2, 20, 22, 29, 32, 81, 82, 86, 102, 110, 114, 116, 121, 123, 124, 125, 131
republicanism, 2, 80, 83, 121, 127
respect, 10
revolution, 16
rights, 1, 2, 6, 7, 8, 9, 10, 11, 12, 13, 15, 16, 22, 23, 27, 33, 34, 43, 80, 81, 82, 104, 112, 133, 135
Rights of Man and Citizen, 9
Roland, Manon, 1, 5, 74, 93, 94, 123, 129
Rousseau, Jean-Jacques, 10, 11, 31, 32, 33, 40, 45, 49, 74, 86, 93, 94, 95, 96, 105, 106, 117, 119, 124, 127, 131, 139

school, 3, 4, 5, 17, 24, 36, 39, 65, 66, 67, 71, 74, 81, 82, 83, 84, 85, 86, 88, 97, 99, 101, 104, 114, 120, 121, 127, 130, 134, 135, 139
self-deception, 56
Sen, Amartya, 44
sisters, 3, 24, 31, 86, 92, 103, 104, 105, 106, 107, 140
slavery, 2, 15, 16, 22, 27, 28, 29, 30, 31, 32, 71, 87
slaves, 15, 16, 27, 28, 30, 45, 70, 87, 125, 133
society, 9, 13, 14, 15, 16, 23, 25, 30, 33, 41, 42, 49, 67, 68, 70, 71, 75, 79, 81, 86, 90, 98, 103, 106, 108, 112, 116, 118, 119, 124, 125, 127, 135, 137, 138, 139
Solanas, Valerie, 7, 136, 137, 141
submission, 39
superiority, 33, 36, 62, 119, 140
syphilis, 16, 75, 76

Taylor, Harriet, 21
teach, 11, 46, 66, 88, 90, 92, 120, 124, 134
teachers, 65, 81, 84, 85, 104, 139
teaching, 11, 20, 65, 83, 85, 97, 101, 106, 107, 121, 137
Thoughts on the Education of Daughters, 4
trades, 99, 101
translation, 30
travel, 48
tyranny, 71, 80, 81, 82, 84, 87, 120, 124, 130, 135

universalism, 14

Vindication of the Rights of Woman, 1, 6, 8, 9, 12, 17, 19, 23, 25, 26, 27, 28, 30, 33, 36, 39, 43, 44, 61, 96, 101, 102, 118, 120, 121, 133
virtue, 10, 11, 12, 13, 15, 16, 22, 23, 24, 25, 30, 32, 40, 43, 44, 45, 52, 54, 90, 98, 103, 111, 112, 114, 116, 120, 122, 133, 135, 136, 140
virtuous, 11, 12, 24, 29, 30, 40, 41, 45, 52, 61, 73, 98, 101, 112, 114, 115, 116, 122, 123, 124, 125, 129, 134, 135

weakness, 17
wife, 30, 40, 42, 43, 47, 49, 57, 75, 80, 86, 92, 93, 94, 96, 97, 98, 103, 108, 111, 140
woman, 3, 5, 7, 12, 14, 17, 20, 21, 22, 24, 26, 31, 32, 34, 36, 37, 40, 42, 43, 48, 49, 51, 54, 55, 56, 57, 58, 59, 62, 63, 65, 68, 69, 70, 71, 73, 75, 78, 88, 90, 91, 92, 94, 95, 97, 98, 99, 101, 102, 103, 106, 109, 110, 111, 112, 118, 133, 135, 137
women, 1, 2, 3, 4, 6, 8, 9, 10, 11, 12, 13, 14, 15, 16, 17, 18, 19, 20, 21, 22, 23, 24, 25, 26, 27, 28, 31,

32, 33, 34, 35, 36, 37, 39, 40, 41, 42, 43, 44, 45, 46, 49, 50, 51, 52, 53, 54, 56, 57, 58, 61, 62, 63, 64, 65, 66, 67, 68, 69, 70, 71, 72, 73, 74, 75, 76, 78, 79, 90, 91, 92, 93, 94, 95, 96, 97, 98, 99, 100, 101, 102, 104, 105, 106, 107, 108, 109, 110, 111, 112, 120, 121, 122, 125, 130, 131, 134, 135, 136, 137, 138, 139, 140, 141

Woolf, Virginia, 22

work, vi, 3, 7, 8, 10, 14, 17, 18, 20, 21, 22, 24, 25, 26, 28, 35, 47, 49, 59, 73, 80, 81, 85, 89, 92, 95, 97, 98, 100, 101, 103, 104, 106, 107, 108, 109, 110, 112, 114, 115, 117, 118, 120, 121, 122, 124, 126, 127, 129, 131, 136, 137, 139, 141

zombies, 120

For EU product safety concerns, contact us at Calle de José Abascal, 56–1°,
28003 Madrid, Spain or eugpsr@cambridge.org.

www.ingramcontent.com/pod-product-compliance
Lightning Source LLC
LaVergne TN
LVHW011835060526
838200LV00053B/4030